Diercke Geography
For Bilingual Classes

Volume 2

Workbook

Moderation:
Prof. Dr. Reinhard Hoffmann

Autorinnen und Autoren:
Sarah Flöck
Henriette Heß
Reinhard Hoffmann
Verena Hundertmark
Marjana Mehltretter
Dirk Reischauer
Ingo Warken

unter Mitwirkung der Verlagsredaktion

westermann

CARL DIERCKE (geb. in Kyritz, Landkreis Ostprignitz/Preußen) lebte von 1842 bis 1913 und war Pädagoge und Kartograph.

Von ihm stammt der bekannte *Diercke-Schulatlas*, der erstmals 1883 unter dem Namen „*Schul-Atlas über alle Teile der Erde*" erschien.

Weitere Informationen finden sich im Internet: *www.diercke.de (Info/Chronik)*

Zur Arbeit mit diesem Buch

Atlashinweise: Schlage den Atlas auf der angegebenen Seite auf oder gib den Karten-Code im Suchfeld der Internet-Adresse ein:

Blaues Symbol: Diercke Weltatlas

100800-240
schueler.diercke.de

DE-172
www.diercke.com

Gelbes Symbol: Diercke International Atlas

↗ *Starthilfe*: Für verschiedene Aufgaben in diesem Workbook findest du hilfreiche Hinweise im Anhang.

Nutze auch die Sprachhilfen am Rand des Workbooks, wenn du mit einer Aufgabe Schwierigkeiten hast.

Methodenhilfe: Hilfestellungen zu den einzelen Arbeitsmethoden, die im Workbook gebraucht werden, findest du auf
€ den Methodenseiten deines Textbooks oder
€ im Abschnitt 'Geo Skills' im TOOLKIT (978-3-14-114042-2).

westermann GRUPPE

© 2017 Bildungshaus Schulbuchverlage
Westermann Schroedel Diesterweg Schöningh Winklers GmbH, Braunschweig
www.westermann.de

Druck A[1] / Jahr 2017
Alle Drucke der Serie A sind im Unterricht parallel verwendbar.
Redaktion: Lars Büttner
Bildredaktion: Susanne Guse
Umschlaggestaltung: Thomas Schröder
Druck und Bindung: westermann druck GmbH, Braunschweig

ISBN 978-3-14-**114040**-8

Contents

Globalisation – What Does It Mean?

1 Describe one of the photos on pages 8 and 9 of your textbook in detail.

_____

_____

_____

_____

_____

_____

_____

_____

_____

_____

_____

_____

_____

_____

to chat   meeting
keyboard   container   dockside crane
to load/unload
screen
container vessel

traveller   check-in desk   amusement park
information screen   Chinese script
gateway
welcome sign   to queue

2 Explain which aspects of globalisation are shown in the photo you have chosen in task 1.

_____

_____

_____

_____

_____

_____

_____

_____

_____

**HELPFUL WORDS
AND PHRASES**
for TASK 2:

- The photo mainly
  shows/depicts/displays
  cultural/political …
  aspects.
- It can be seen that …
- It gives a good
  overview of …
- It shows/provides
  many details of …
- The main aspect is …
- An additional point is …

Globalisation

 100800-268, -282
schueler.diercke.de

 DE-194, - 196
www.diercke.com

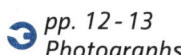 *pp. 12 - 13*
Photographs

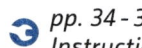 *pp. 34 - 35*
Instructions

Globalisation or 'The World is Shrinking'

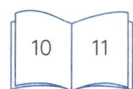

In 1492, Christopher Columbus set sail and travelled west in order to reach the East Indies. Accidentally, he stumbled across landmasses unknown at that time: the New World. He stumbled because the Earth is not flat, it is a sphere. This momentous accident is labelled 'Globalization 1.0' by Thomas Friedman in 'The World Is Flat', and it marks the beginning of the era of 'countries globalizing'. In the nineteenth and twentieth centuries, transport and communication technology made fast progress, leading the world into an era of 'companies globalising', 'Globalization 2.0'. Finally, starting around the year 2000, Friedman defines the current era as 'Globalization 3.0', which is built around individuals.

Besides the fact that the Earth is a sphere, its size started growing: the Americas – and later Australia – had to be added to the maps of the Earth one after the other. While the Earth seemed to be growing, technological progress and the smartest people on the planet were constantly working to make the Earth smaller and smaller.

While sailing away from the Old World, Columbus was sailing towards the New World. The growth of the Internet works quite like this: every additional connection adds new users. These users can access the knowledge and information of the rest of the Internet and vice versa. The growing Web brings people closer together and makes the world a smaller place.

Globalisation today is intrinsically tied to the Internet. Due to the fact that we have accomplished many things since its development, people often state that the idea of global Internet access, no matter how far off a place is, will be best for all. However, it is forgotten that the Internet is not mainly used to do good or to help people in need. Most people use their smartphones and notebooks to access social media in order to get unimportant or even useless information.

In German the term 'Smombie' (a combination of smartphone and zombie) is a good description of the state many people are in while online.

Still, when used in reference to globalisation, the Internet truly has its upside: there are encyclopaedias where people can share and obtain information on everything they could probably think of, for instance. But there also is a dark side of the Internet: free speech easily becomes hate speech in social media, people can easily be badmouthed, and extremists of all shades can recruit and share their sick worldviews with their (soon-to-be) followers. The Internet is a brilliant creation, as is globalisation. Both have unimaginable potential, and both are wasted on things either dumbing and numbing people into zombie-like mobile phone addicts, or benefitting only a certain few.

There are as many faces of the Internet as there are of globalisation. Accidentally, both are filled and defined, for example, by music, art, religion, food, and people. There will always be people aiming at the end of progress of globalisation – interestingly using one of its most important tools for their own needs.

It is true: globalisation can be a monster. It is on all of us to turn it into our saviour by using global cooperation as a tool of freedom and global progress.

1 Summarize the main idea of each text in not more than 75 words.

2 Explain the two views of globalisation and the role of the Internet that are presented in the texts.

3 Comment on the role of the Internet in the process of globalisation.

100800-268, -270
schueler.diercke.de

DE-194
www.diercke.com

pp. 32 - 33
Texts

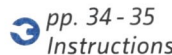
pp. 34 - 35
Instructions

5

Transport in a 'Shrinking World'

1 Show the development of today's leading cargo and passenger airports (›textbook: p. 13) in two diagrams.

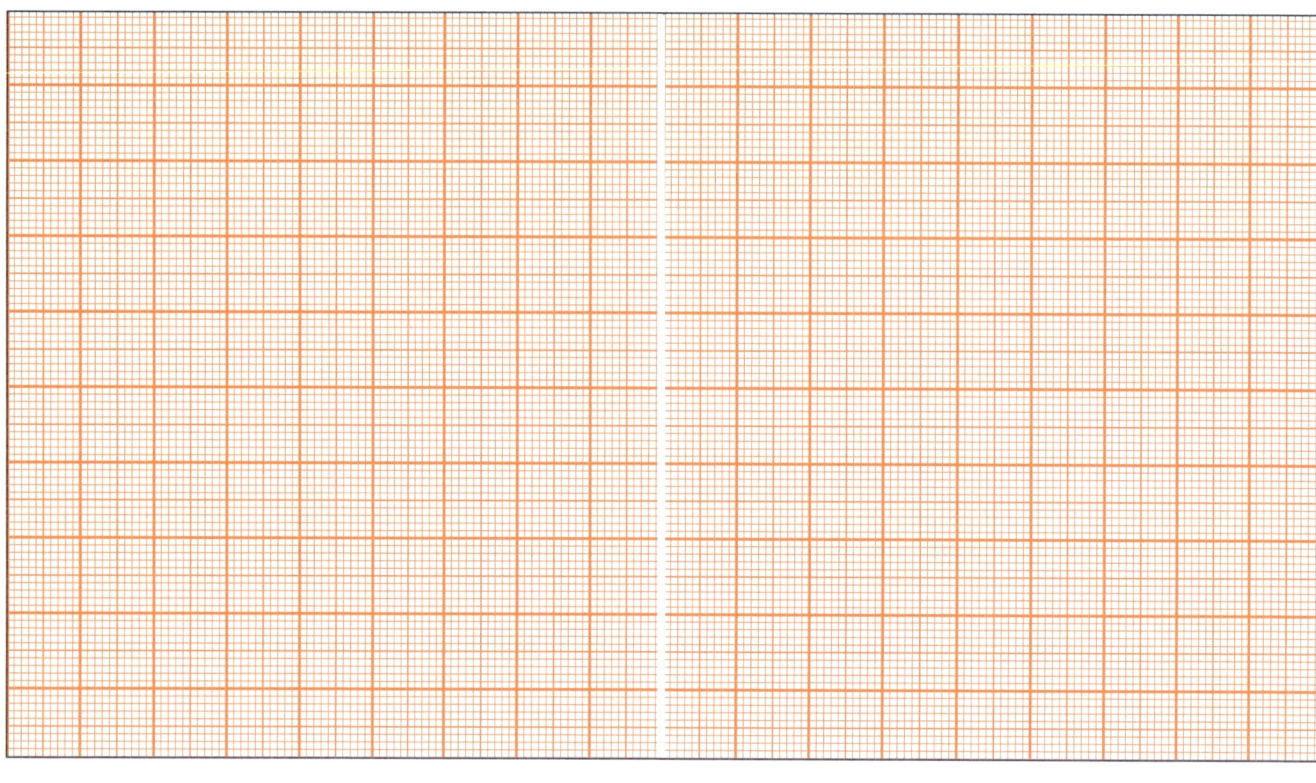

2 Describe the development of cargo volume and passenger numbers of the airports listed from 2005 to 2015.

_____

_____

_____

_____

_____

3 Compare the development of cargo volume and the development of passenger numbers of the airports listed between 2005 and 2015.

_____

_____

_____

_____

_____

Globalisation

 100800-268, -272
schueler.diercke.de

 DE-194
www.diercke.com

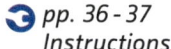 pp. 36 - 37
Instructions

Information and Communication Technology Changes Life

1 Describe the pictures shown in M1 (›textbook p. 14) in detail.

_____

_____

_____

_____

_____

_____

_____

_____

_____

_____

_____

_____

_____

_____

shorts traditional jewellery traditional tattoos flip-flops online business meeting stump texting bare upper body screen videoconference handheld device office laptop feather headdress

2 Explain how information and communication technology connects people around the world with the help of these pictures.

_____

_____

_____

_____

_____

_____

_____

_____

100800-268, -282
schueler.diercke.de
DE-194, - 196
www.diercke.com
pp. 12 - 13 Photographs
pp. 34 - 35 Instructions

7

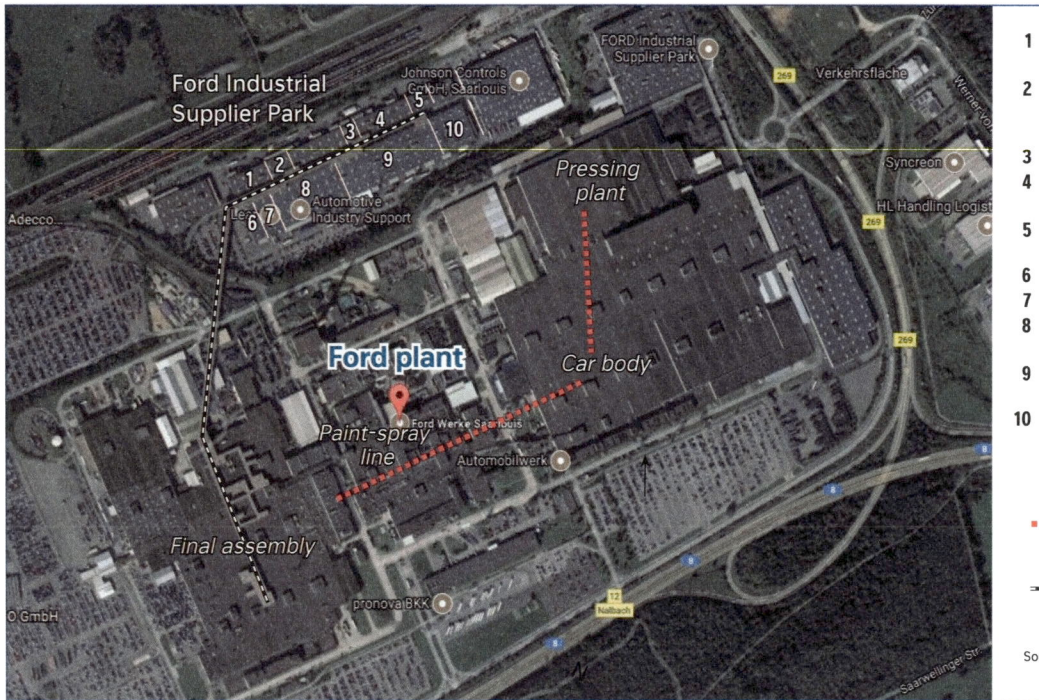

1 Glazier's workshop
  Verglasung
2 Cockpit and radiator modules
  Cockpit- und Kühlermodul
3 Metalwork
4 Exhaust system
  Abgasanlage
5 Hardware and software solutions
6 Door and side covering
7 Roof interior module
8 Main wiring loom
  Hauptkabelstrang
9 Engine and gearbox pre-assembly
10 Front and rear suspension module
  Vorder- und Hinterachs-modul

▪▪▪▪▪ Production flow of assembly inside the plant
▬▬▬ Fixed transport link

Source (Satellite image): Google Maps

12708EX_1

M1 Ford plant in Saarlouis, Germany (setup and its industrial supplier park)

1 Explain the production process in the Ford plant in Saarlouis using the terms outsourcing / in-house production depth / just-in-time.

_____

_____

_____

_____

_____

_____

_____

Ford in Deutschland

Das Ford-Werk Saarlouis ist Impulsgeber und Wachstumsmotor für das Saarland. Hier wurden bisher schon mehr als 12 Millionen Ford-Modelle gefertigt – und es werden täglich mehr. Damit zählt das Werk zu den effizientesten und produktivsten Automobilwerken in Europa.

Der Industriekomplex rund um Ford ist der größte Arbeitgeber des Saarlandes. Rund 6.500 Menschen arbeiten direkt für Ford, dazu kommen 2.000 Arbeitsplätze bei den Zulieferern des Unternehmens. Insgesamt sind in Saarlouis 14 Zulieferer direkt im Industriepark oder in der Nähe ansässig.

Source: www.ford.de (2017)

M2 Information about the plant

_____

_____

_____

_____

_____

_____

_____

_____

 100800-268 schueler.diercke.de

 DE-194 www.diercke.com

↻ *pp. 14-15 Aerial Photographs*

↻ *pp. 34-35 Instructions*

Globalisation

Location Factors

1. Rate the importance of the given location factors for the choice of a site for
   a) the research and development of a new smartphone.
   b) the final assembly of a smartphone.
   Use the diagrams to rate the importance of the location factors (1 = not very important; 5 = extremely important). Connect the marks you have made in each diagram with a line.

2. Give reasons for your choice next to the diagrams.

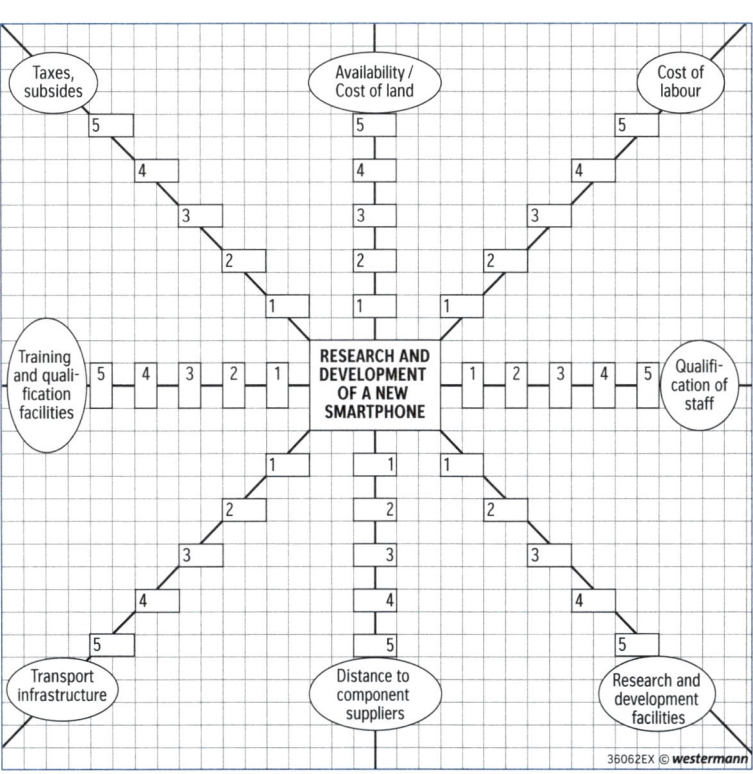

M1 Diagram for a) – research and development (R&D)

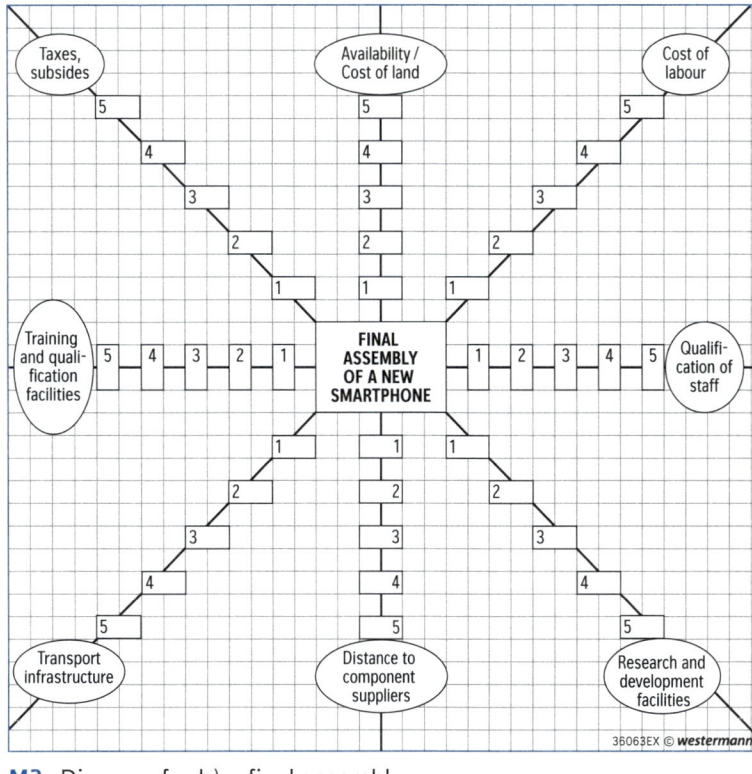

M2 Diagram for b) – final assembly

9

World Trade

❶ Are the following statements true or false? Tick the correct boxes with the help of your textbook.

Structure	True?	False?
1. Germany does not export any raw material as one of its top five products.		
2. Most raw materials are exported to North America, Europe, and Australia.		
3. There are no European countries which mainly export raw materials.		
4. Most African countries export raw materials (mainly or as one of their top five export products).		
5. Soy beans are among the main raw materials exported from African countries.		
6. Cotton is a highly important export material for Mali.		
7. Oil and natural gas are among Canada's top five export products.		
8. China and the USA do not have raw materials, so they cannot export any.		
9. Oil is the most important raw material exported from the Arabian peninsula and Northern Africa.		
10. Between 2010 and 2015, 1,000 litres of crude oil were more expensive than a car.		
11. Crude oil and coffee show a high variability in prices, whereas the price of cars is rising quite constantly.		

❷ Germany and Japan are two highly industrialised countries. Describe from where companies in these two countries import raw materials. Use your atlas.

German companies:

_____

_____

_____

_____

_____

_____

Japanese companies:

_____

_____

_____

_____

_____

 100800-266, -268
schueler.diercke.de

 DE-194
www.diercke.com

➌ *pp. 4-5*
Atlas

Globalisation – Worldwide Differences

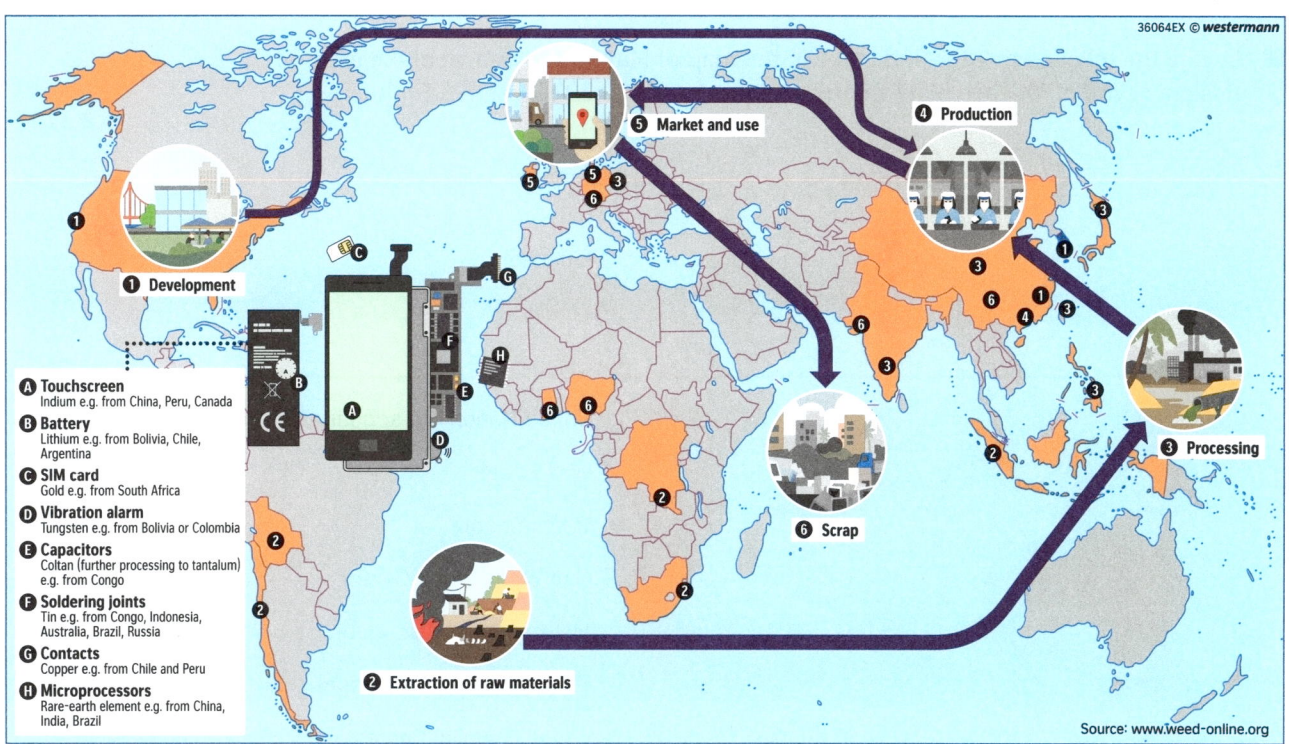

36064EX © *westermann*

A Touchscreen
Indium e.g. from China, Peru, Canada

B Battery
Lithium e.g. from Bolivia, Chile, Argentina

C SIM card
Gold e.g. from South Africa

D Vibration alarm
Tungsten e.g. from Bolivia or Colombia

E Capacitors
Coltan (further processing to tantalum) e.g. from Congo

F Soldering joints
Tin e.g. from Congo, Indonesia, Australia, Brazil, Russia

G Contacts
Copper e.g. from Chile and Peru

H Microprocessors
Rare-earth element e.g. from China, India, Brazil

❶ Development
❷ Extraction of raw materials
❸ Processing
❹ Production
❺ Market and use
❻ Scrap

Source: www.weed-online.org

1. Development Development and design takes place where the company has its headquarters (e.g. in USA). The company then commissions contracting firms to produce the different components (e.g. in China).	**4. Production** Single components are assembled to a smartphone by contract manufacturers (e.g. in China). Although this production is an important economic factor and creates jobs, often e.g. working conditions are bad.
2. Extraction of raw materials Raw materials are extracted in different countries. In some mines (e.g. in Congo), people have to face bad working and living conditions as well as child labour.	**5. Market and use** The assembled smartphone is delivered to retailers all over the world and, from there, sold to consumers.
3. Processing Raw materials are processed to single components. Manufacturing and assembly of components take place in e.g. China, Vietnam or India.	**6. Scrap** Worldwide, every fifth person owns a smartphone and the average service life of a smartphone is 18 months. Therefore, a lot of electronic waste is produced that needs to be recycled to avoid environmental pollution.

M1 Global production of a smartphone

❶ Describe the global production of a smartphone (**M1**).

_____

_____

_____

_____

_____

_____

❷ Explain global fragmentation using global production as an example (**M1**).

 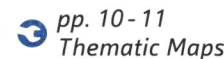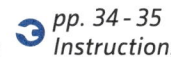

New York – A Global City

1 Locate the following places and areas in the map of Manhattan and label the map (**M1**). Assign a symbol for each place or area. Use your atlas and the Internet for help.

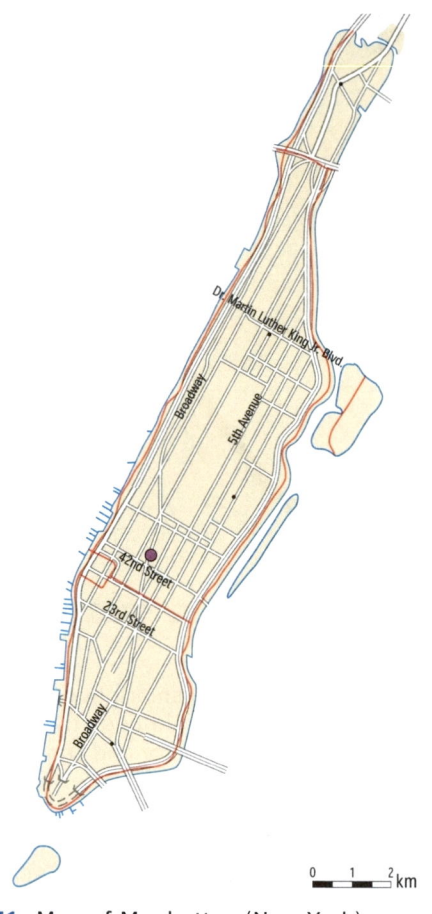

M1 Map of Manhattan (New York)

Key / Symbol:

Little Italy

Koreatown

Chinatown

United Nations Headquarters

Wall Street

● Times Square

One World Trade Center

Metropolitan Museum of Art

The Guggenheim Museum

World Financial Center

36065EX © *westermann*

2 Make a mind map about the topic 'Manhattan – centre of a global city'. Use the text in your textbook.

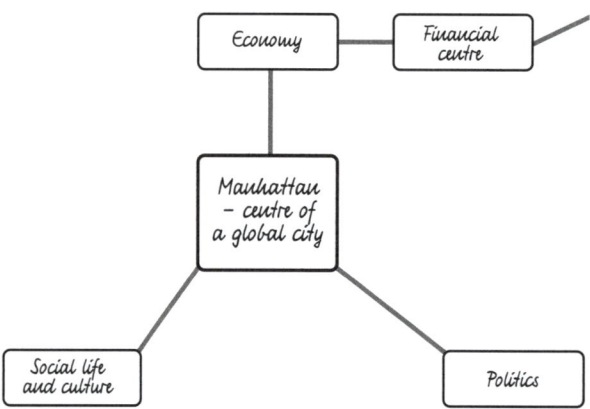

Global Disparities

100800-218, -219
schueler.diercke.de

DE-142
www.diercke.com

↻ pp. 32-33
Texts

Land reclamation – a closer look

1 Describe land reclamation in Singapore with the help of **M1**, **M2** and your textbook (›p.29: **M4**).

_____

_____

_____

_____

_____

_____

_____

_____

_____

_____

_____

_____

M1 Land reclamation near Tekong Island/ Singapore

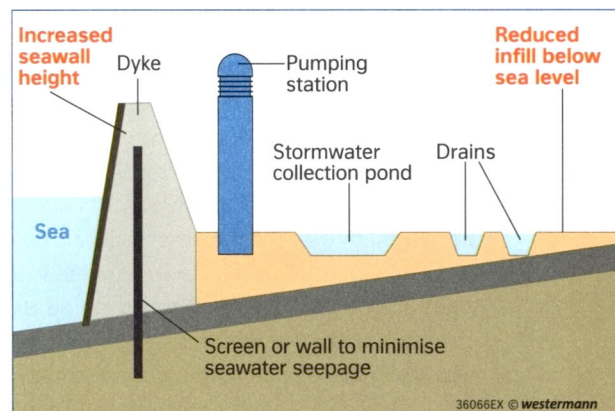

M2 The empoldering method

2 Explain why Singapore has been using land reclamation. Use selected facts from **M3**.

_____

_____

_____

_____

_____

_____

_____

_____

_____

_____

_____

_____

_____

Land reclamation

- start of land reclamation in the early 19th century; on a large scale since the 1960s
- increase of total land area from 581.5 km^2 (1960) to 719.7 km^2 (2016)
- massive increase in population from 1.6 million people (1960) to 5.6 million (2016)
- growing economy
- country in need of space for housing and the expansion of industrial and transport facilities, including the port
- land reclamation started in swamps during the colonial period, later along the coast and offshore islands
- problems due to technological limits, high costs and limited resources of sand
- dispute with neighbouring country Malaysia over territories

M3 Background information

 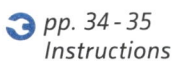

The two Detroits: a city both collapsing and gentrifying at the same time

In the late 1980s, James Cadariu's family fled for the suburbs, part of the massive "white flight" that helped turn Detroit from a bustling city of two million into a city of under 700,000. Cadariu, now 44, came back and co-owns Great Lakes Coffee Roasting Company, which has a retail outlet[1] on Woodward Ave in Midtown and sells fairtrade coffee. It sits across from a Whole Foods, down the street from a craft brewery[2] and right along the M-1, a new streetcar line that will connect midtown with downtown – two neighbourhoods that have seen their fortunes rise as Detroit emerges from bankruptcy and attracts new businesses, infrastructure and residents at rates not seen in decades.

"I've seen Detroit as a large city. I've seen it decline," Cadariu said. "But I've never seen as much growth downtown as I do now." [...]

And then there's the rest of Detroit. In the neighbourhoods outside the downtown core, residents earn an average of 25% less. Housing is crumbling.[3] There are 150,000 vacant or abandoned buildings. [...]

Separated by as little as a city block, the new Detroit and the rest of Detroit feel like two completely different cities – physically close, far apart in everything else: education, income, outlook on their future. [...] Where there's been a confluence[4] of public incentives[5] and private investment, Detroit is booming. In the rest of Detroit the chasm[6] between rich and poor is growing. [...]

[Investors] of Detroit, along with the leaders of the car companies and the nonprofits they fund, have used their influence to build billions of dollars' worth of infrastructure. Detroit is 138.7 square miles big, but the vast majority of the new money that has poured[7] into the city has pooled in the 7.2 square miles of downtown. [...] The infrastructure has spurred[8] a real estate boom. Vacancy rates in the core are mostly under 5%. Tech startups are plentiful. Artists are being lured[9] by cheap rent. Small manufacturers are moving in, and big companies are offering incentives for their young employees to live in the city centre. Developers argue that it's just a matter of time before other neighbourhoods rise up, too. [...]

Jocelyn Harris has lived in one of those "challenged" outer Detroit neighborhoods, about six miles east of downtown, all her life. Her house is one of the only occupied properties on her block. [...] "We used to have everything: department stores, grocery stores, all of it," Harris said. "Now the sewage backs up, the park is locked, the school is closed". [...]

Part of the knock-on impact is that residents of these under-serviced areas aren't ready to take advantage of jobs coming to the city. Residents of Detroit's outer neighbourhoods are not only poorer and worse-prepared for jobs than those in the core, but young people are about four times less likely to be college educated.

Source: www.guardian.com (05 Feb 2015, abridged)

M1 Excerpt from a newspaper article

❶ Characterise the 'two Detroits' as depicted in the article.

HELPFUL WORDS
for M1:
1 – Einzelhandelsgeschäft
2 – Bierbrauerei
3 – zerbröckeln
4 – zusammenfließen
5 – Impulse
6 – Kluft
7 – gießen
8 – beleben, anregen
9 – ködern, anziehen

pp. 32 - 33
Texts

Global Disparities

M1 Up to 1,500 fishermen and businessmen, who try to make their living catching Nile Perch, live on the tiny island of Migingo in Lake Victoria

Lake Victoria – Once the Rich Fishing Grounds

1 Show the changes in Lake Victoria and fill in the flow chart.
Fill in the missing words from the list in the boxes below. Use your textbook for help.

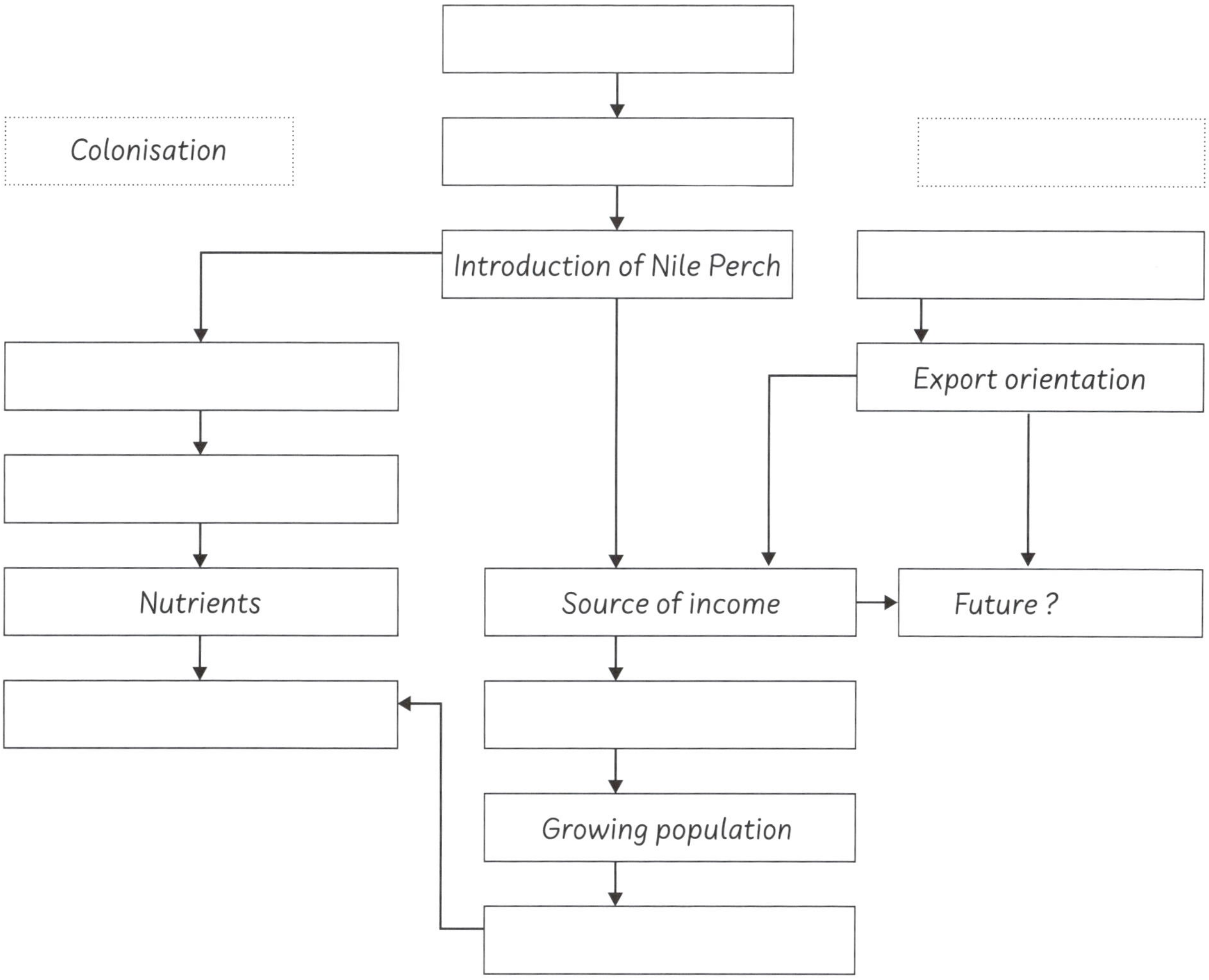

Colonisation

Introduction of Nile Perch

Export orientation

Nutrients

Source of income

Future ?

Growing population

Globalisation   Growing demand for Nile Perch   Overfishing of Nile Perch
Spread of plankton   Extinction of native fish species   Deforestation/Waste
Growing population   Overfishing   Decline of water quality   Migrant workers

36067EX © *westermann*

 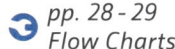

Shanghai – A Fast Changing City

Population development of Shanghai/China

Year	Population in million
1980	6.0
1990	7.8
2000	14.0
2010	20.0
2020*	27.2
2030*	30.8

Source: www.statista.com (2016, *Prognosis)

M1 Population development of Shanghai

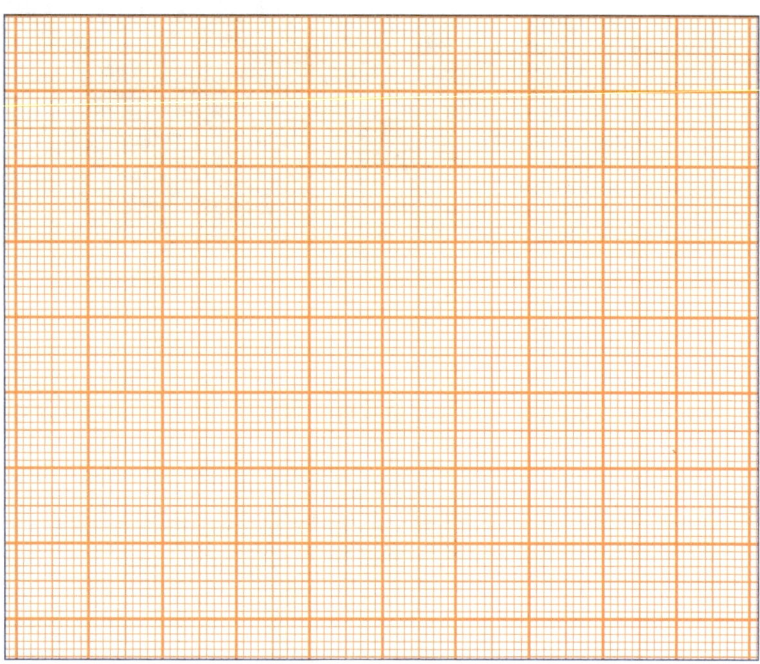

❶ Draw a line graph using the population numbers of Shanghai (**M1**).

❷ Describe the population development of Shanghai between 1980 and 2030.

❸ Give reasons for this development and discuss the estimates for the future population growth of Shanghai. Use your textbook.

_____

_____

_____

_____

_____

_____

_____

_____

_____

_____

_____

_____

Global Disparities

16
 100800-189 schueler.diercke.de
 DE-108 www.diercke.com
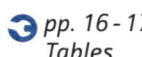 pp. 16-17 Tables
pp. 18-19 Line Graphs

Level of Development and Indicators

Indicator	Country A	Country B	Country C	Country D
GNP per capita (current international US-$)	49,040	14,280	3,290	6,050
GDP, by sector of origin (in %): agriculture/industry/services	0.6/30.3/69.1	5.3/22.7/72.0	26.7/29.8/43.5	16.5/29.8/53.7
Total fertility rate (children born/woman)	1.44	1.76	2.56	2.45
Life expectancy (total, in years)	80.70	73.80	64.50	68.50
Literacy rate (total, in %)	99.00	92.60	73.80	72.20
Physicians per 1,000 inhabitants	4.13	1.85	0.17	0.73
Label				

Source: CIA Factbook, World Bank (2015)

M1 Structural data of different countries

❶ a) Characterise the stage of development of countries A-D (**M1**).
b) Label the countries as MEDC, LEDC or NIC.

❷ Compare the stage of development of countries A-D (**M1**).

 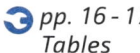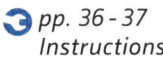

Globalisation – Different Views

M1 Cartoon

❶ Find a headline for the cartoon (**M1**).

_____

❷ Analyse the cartoon (**M1**).

CHECKLIST
for TASK 2:
Have you ...
• ... described the cartoon systemati-cally? ☐
• ... interpreted the information of the cartoon? ☐
• ... analysed the cartoonist's message? ☐
• ... stated your opinion? ☐

_____

_____

_____

_____

_____

_____

_____

_____

_____

_____

_____

_____

pp. 154 - 155
Cartoons   pp. 30 - 31
Cartoons

Global Disparities

World Population

1 Note down the key term for the following definitions:

ⓐ *The number of births to a woman aged 15 to 45:* _____

ⓑ *The number of deaths per thousand of the population per year:* _____

ⓒ *The number of live births per thousand of the population per year:* _____

ⓓ *The difference between c and b:* _____

ⓔ *The development of the number of people due to natural increase or decrease, and migration:* _____

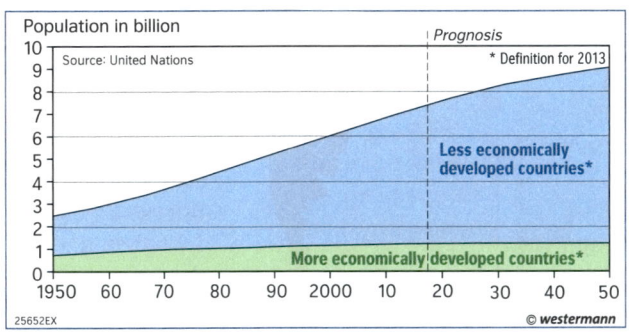

M1 World population development

M2 Rate of natural increase

2 Fill in the gaps with the help of **M1** and **M2**.

Over the past sixty years, the world's population has seen a dramatic increase, from _____ people in 1950

to around _____ in 2015, with almost all of the population growth occurring in _____ countries.

This trend is projected to continue: by 2050 the world's population is expected to reach _____ ,

of which only ten per cent will live in _____ countries. This rapid growth in the world population

has occurred despite a marked _____ in the world population growth rate due to falling fertility

rates. With two per cent, the worldwide growth rate reached its peak in the _____ and has fallen shar-

ply since then. In 2005, it stood at _____ per cent and is expected to drop further to about _____ per

cent by 2045. The world's total population is still _____ , however, because of the large number

of women of childbearing age in developing countries.

3 Give reasons for the high birth rates in developing countries.

4 Fill in the table **M3** with the help of the Internet:
http://www.worldometers.info/

Date of access	
The current world population	
Net population growth this year	

M3 World population

The Demographic Transition Model

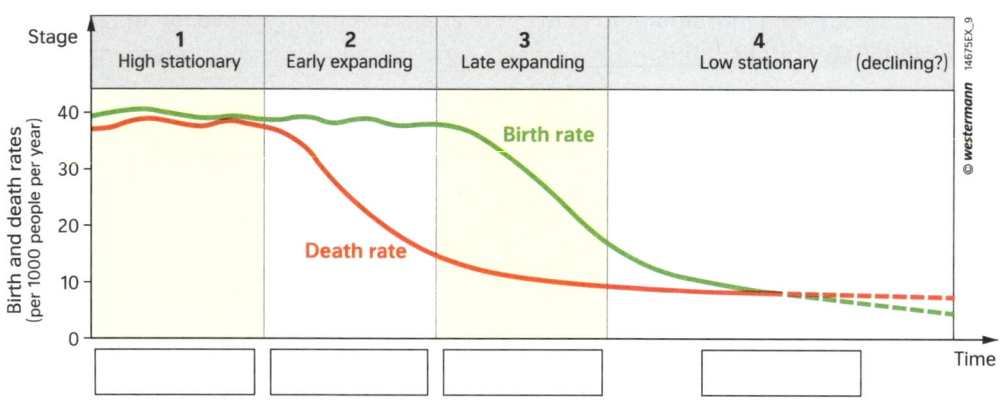

M1 Demographic Transition Model (DTM)

1. High (30-40/1,000 inhabitants) due to diseases, famine, lack of clean drinking water and health care.

2. Low (10/1,000 inhabitants), in some states even falling below the death rate, as a result of a high marital age. Families do not have more children than they want to have.

3. Low, due to good health care and medical advances, access to clean water and good food supply. It can rise again because of a high proportion of older inhabitants.

4. High (30-40/1,000 inhabitants) due to lack of family planning, low marital age and poor school education. Children contribute to the family income.

5. Sinking, due to improved health care, advances in hygiene and better food and water supply. In particular, the infant mortality decreases.

6. Sinking, as a result of an improved status of women, access to contraceptives, familiy planning, and a higher marital age.

❶ a) Match the numbers in the boxes with the appropriate stages of the Demographic Transition Model (**M1**).
   Note: The colours of the boxes correspond to the colours of the lines in the diagram.
   b) Draw the rate of natural increase into the diagram above.
   c) Describe the population development for each stage.

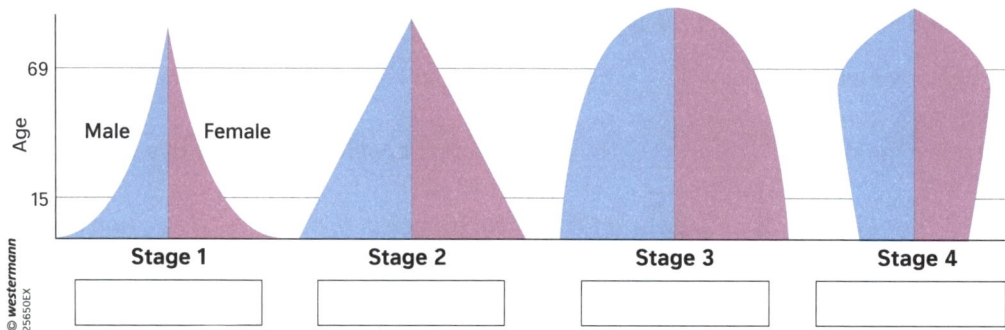

M2 Typical shapes of age-and-gender diagrams

❷ Match the age-and-gender diagrams (**M2**) with the statements below.

1. The birth rate rapidly falls. The death rate falls. The population growth is high. More people live to be older.
2. Birth and death rates are high. The population growth is close to zero. The life expectancy is low (few people reach old age), so the population is made up of mostly young people.
3. The birth rate is very low. The death rate is low. The population growth is zero or negative. The life expectancy is high. There are more older people than young people.
4. The birth rate is high. The death rate falls and the population growth rate is very high. The life expectancy has increased, and there are still more younger and than older people.

People

100800-276
schueler.diercke.de

DE-190
www.diercke.com

pp. 152-153
Age-and-Gender

pp. 24-25
Age-and-Gender

The Challenges of Population Change

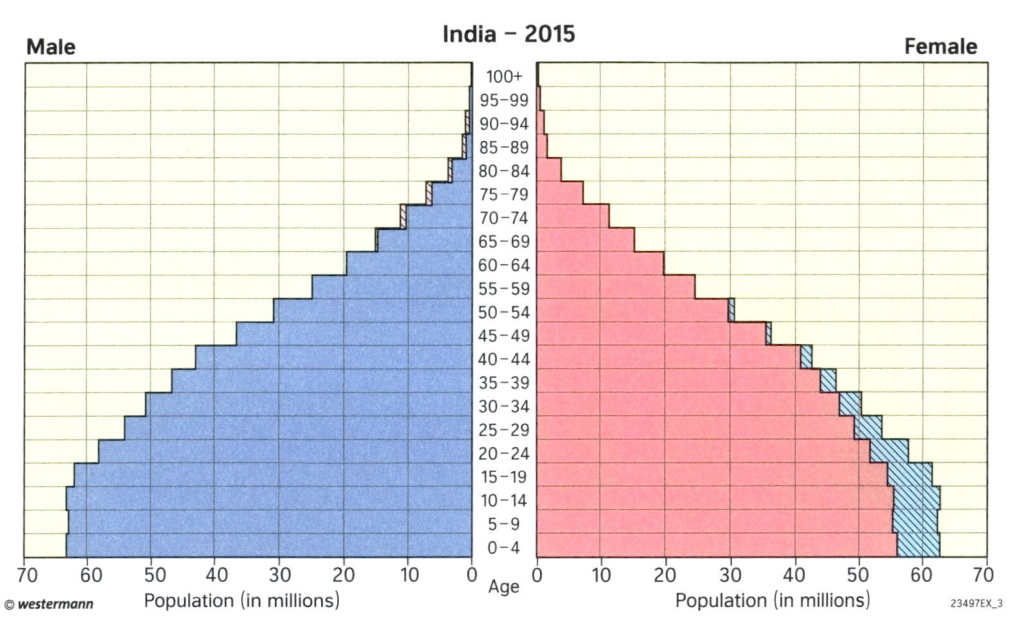

Male **India – 2015** **Female**

© westermann   Population (in millions)   Age   Population (in millions)   23497EX_3

M1 Age-and-gender diagram of India

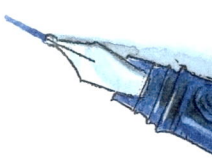

❶ Describe the age-and-gender diagram of India (**M1**).

_____

_____

_____

_____

_____

_____

❷ Determine whether the population structure represents that of a more or less economically developed country (MEDC or a LEDC). Give reasons for your opinion.

India is a: _____

Reasons: _____

_____

❸ Name strategies to meet the challenges of population change in India. Answer in English or German.

_____

_____

_____

_____

↻ pp. 152-153   ↻ pp. 24-25
Age-and-Gender   Age-and-Gender

Feeding the World

① Write down the most important messages that can be concluded from **M1**.

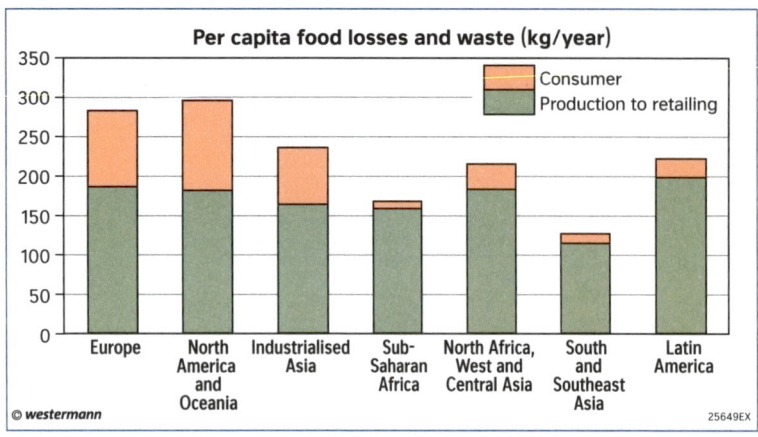

_____

_____

_____

_____

_____

M1 Food losses and waste in different regions

② Keep a log for a week in which you document your food waste:

Day	Kind of food/ amount	Country/ region of origin
Monday		
Tuesday		
Wednesday		
Thursday		
Friday		
Saturday		
Sunday		

③ **REDUCE FOOD WASTE!** – Read the tip of how to reduce food waste. Think of more tips!

Learn when food gets bad. A lot of food can still be consumed even after the expiration date.

_____

_____

④ Make a flyer or poster for a campaign raising awareness to the problem of food waste. Use the information from this page.

 100800-275
schueler.diercke.de
 DE-192
www.diercke.com
➌ *pp. 20 - 21*
Bar Charts

International Migration

1 Read the migrants' stories and fill in the chart below.

Ahmed: 'One night bombs killed 400 people. We left our family home in Aleppo in ruins after it was struck by an explosion. Somehow, I made it to Istanbul. The first weeks were very difficult and lonely. I joined five of my Syrian friends and started working in a factory. It was enough to buy food, but nothing more. So, the six of us decided to seek asylum in the European Union. We left with maps, food and flashlights. We walked for three days until we crossed into Bulgaria. There we were taken to a rundown camp. It was horrible. There were no proper bathrooms and there was very little food.'

Raj: 'I was working for an IT company in California when my boss told me to go to Germany. My job was to expand the German branch of that company in Frankfurt. That was in 1999 – and I'm still here. Germany is a very good place to do business. I have arrived and I live with my family next to Frankfurt. I support social and environmental projects and I often watch the games of our soccer team, the Frankfurter Eintracht.'

Leila: 'Salif and I hope to get married soon. We fled Mali with my father, who refused to let me suffer the traditional practice of being cut[1]. What awaited us in Libya was even worse. My father was killed, and I was raped. We had to leave. We pleaded to be allowed on to a boat headed for Europe, but during the journey an armed gang took all of our water and food. Five people on our boat drowned. Eventually, we were rescued by a German ship and landed in Catania. My first two weeks in Italy were spent in hospital. Now, I finally feel safe.'

Kiran: 'The earthquake reduced most of our family's four-story house in Chautara to rubble. Miraculously, no one was killed when the walls collapsed. I've only been married for six months but I left Nepal almost immediately to work in Portugal. Luckily, I was supported by a Portuguese aid agency. Now I will have to work for many years so we can build again. It is very hard for both of us. I miss her … and want to go home to help our family rebuild. Now we only have Viber (social media) to keep us together.'

Carmen: 'I decided to take my children to America after I couldn't find a job at the local factories. In the past, I worked in Honduras in a factory making bras and panties. I looked all over. I brought my papers to various companies. I have experience but I couldn't find anything. I have two cousins in Dallas, so last month I brought my family to join them. The U.S. is an advanced country, and I want my children to study there. I want them to have a better life.'

M1 Migrants' stories

HELPFUL WORD
for M1:
1 – Genitalbeschneidung

Name	Home country	Push factors	Host country	Pull factors	Current situation
Ahmed					
Raj					
Leila					
Kiran					
Carmen					

 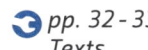

Internal Migration

1 a) Make a diagram that illustrates urbanisation in more and less economically developed countries (MEDCs, LEDCs).

b) Describe and compare the developments shown in you bar chart.

	1950	2000	2050*
MEDC	54.6	74.2	85.5
LEDC	17.7	39.9	63.4

Source: www.statista.com (2016, *Prognosis)

M1 Percentage of urban population in MEDCs and LEDCs

_____

_____

_____

_____

_____

_____

_____

2 Describe the conditions for people who arrive in Kibera to make a living in Nairobi (**M2**, **M3**).

_____

_____

_____

_____

_____

_____

_____

Corrugated-iron shacks

Unpaved road

Lack of water supply

M2 Kibera – informal settlement in Nairobi (Kenya)

Nsulubi Kaburu, 29 years:
'Nairobi was special for the people in my rural area. We thought Nairobi was a clean place with fresh water. Houses in Nairobi were supposed to be of good standards and I even thought I would live in a house next to the president. I was happy when I first came with the bus downtown, but after taking a matatu [local transportation] to Kibera my feelings changed. It was raining, Kibera was muddy and houses were leaking. My first impression of the slum changed me, I was so depressed and for some time I could not eat!'

M3 First impressions of a migrant arriving in Kibera

 100800-279 schueler.diercke.de

 DE-195 www.diercke.com

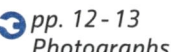 pp. 12-13 Photographs

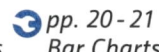 pp. 20-21 Bar Charts

People

Energy – A Vital Component of Our Life

A changing energy consumption worldwide

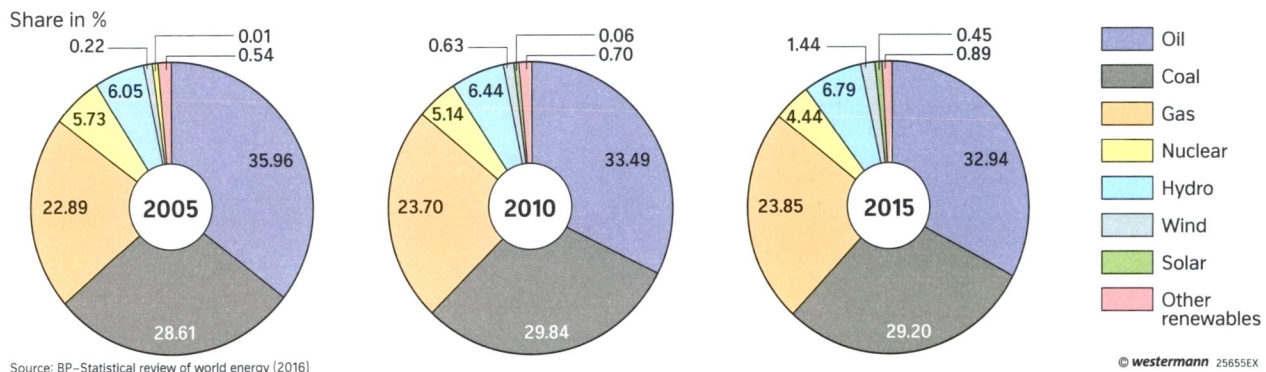

Source: BP–Statistical review of world energy (2016)

© *westermann* 25655EX

M1 Comparative primary energy consumption of the world 2005, 2010 and 2015

1 a) Turn **M1** into a table.

Title: _____

Source: _____

Energy source	2005	2010	2015
total			100.0
total Mtoe*	11,355	12,540	13,423

*megatonnes oil equivalent (unit of energy content)

HELPFUL WORDS
for TASK 1 (b):
- In my view/opinion ...
- I believe/suppose ...
- The material suggests (that) ...

b) Discuss which of the two media (pie chart, table) is better suited for comparison.

2 a) Calculate the absolute energy consumption for oil and wind for the three years (**M1**).

Energy source	2005	2010	2015

b) Discuss the results.

3 Write a short newspaper article about major changes in the world energy consumption in German.

 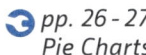

Coal – The Dirty but Indispensable Fuel

Coalification turns plants into coal

Coalification takes place over millions of years. Heat and pressure are the driving forces for the changes from plant to coal.

Dry mass of	% C	% H	% O	Heating value (MJ/kg)	Heating value (% of graphite)
Plant cellulose	45	6	49	10	
Wood	50	6	44	10-11	
Peat	60	6	34	10-12	
Lignite	62	5	33	16-24	
Bituminous coal	79	5	17	26-30	
Anthracite	91	4	5	32-34	
Graphite	100	0	0	34	*100*

M1 Chemical and energetic changes during coalification

1 Calculate the heating value of the different substances in per cent of graphite.

2 Describe the most striking changes taking place in coalification.

3 a) Turn **M1** into a meaningful diagram for a presentation slide.
b) Explain your choice.

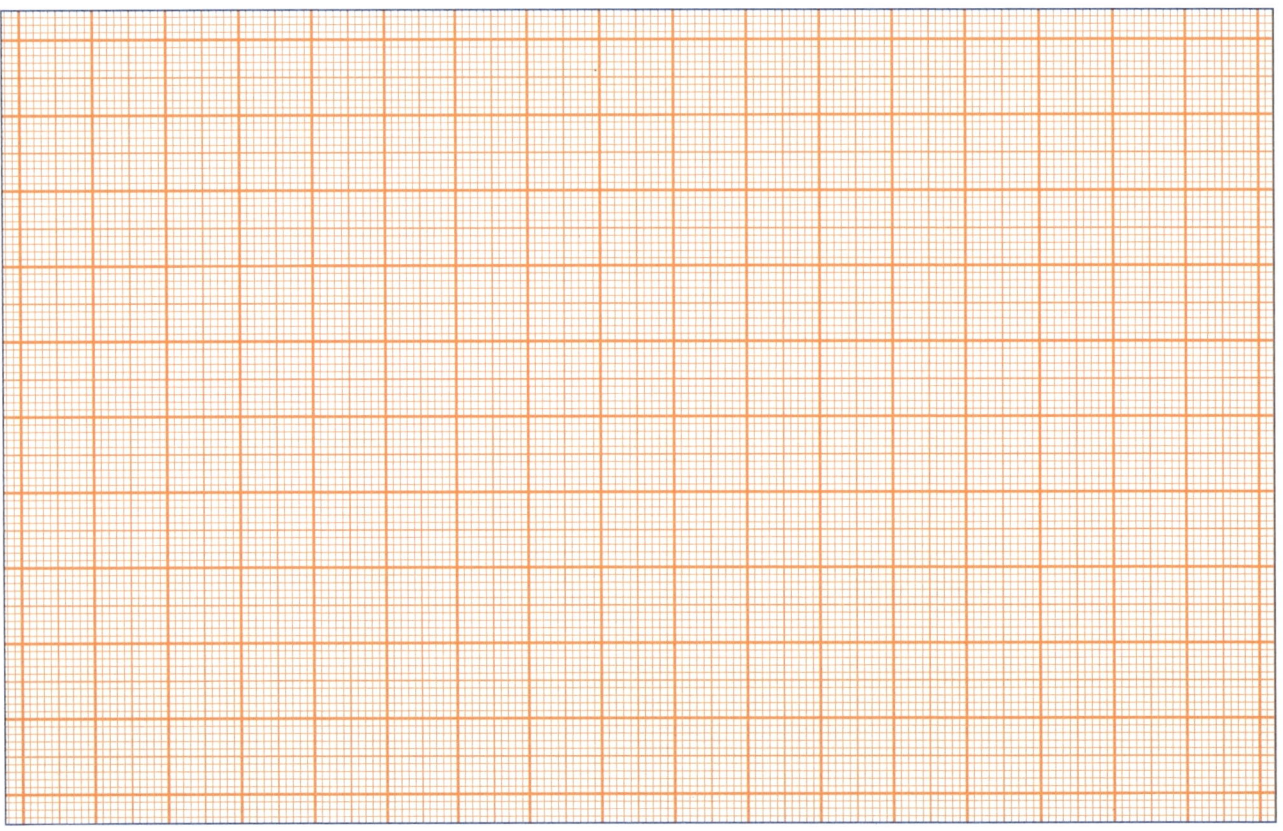

100800-067, -264
schueler.diercke.de

DE-048
www.diercke.com

pp. 16-17
Tables

pp. 20-21
Bar Charts

pp. 34-35
Instructions

Energy Resources

Crude Oil – Still the Black Gold

America's dependency on foreign oil

❶ Describe the global balance of the crude oil trade for North America (**M1**).

❷ Discuss in what way fracking and oil sands might influence the dependency of the region on oil from abroad.

❸ a) Sum up **M2** in three statements.

1. _____

_____

_____

2. _____

_____

_____

3. _____

_____

b) Comment on the necessity of these 'war games'.

A Matter of National Security

The United States would be nearly powerless to protect the US economy if it came to a catastrophic disruption of oil markets, caused by terrorist attacks and political unrest. This was the conclusion by well-known participants in a war game in Washington in June 2005. [...]

The simulation game was organized by two groups that focus on the impact of American dependency on imported oil on national security: the National Commission on Energy Policy and Securing America's Future Energy (SAFE). [...]

The participants concluded that they must urge the president to invest quickly in technologies to reduce the dependency on overseas oil, such as hybrid cars and cars that run on fuels obtained from prairie grasses, animal waste and other seemingly useless but energy-rich products.

M2 After a newspaper article

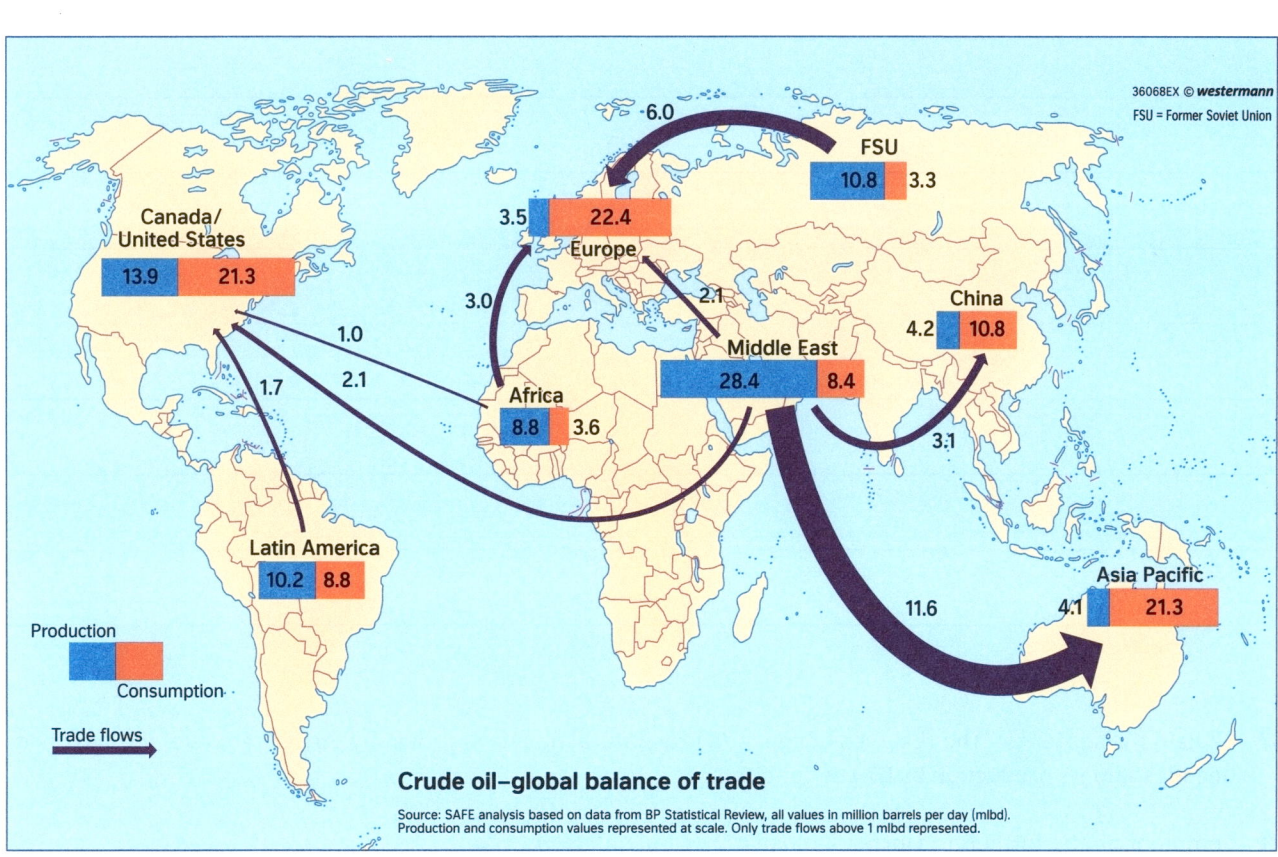

M1 Daily oil trade flows between world regions (2015)

Natural Gas – A Clean Fossil Fuel?

Recent developments in gas reserves

Helpful words for M1:

1 – Turbinen mit mehrfacher Energiegewinnung
2 – Wirkungsgrad
3 – im Voraus
4 – Fortschritte
5 – Ausstattung
6 – Terrakubikmeter

(10^{12} m³; = Billionen Kubikmeter: trillion cubic metres)

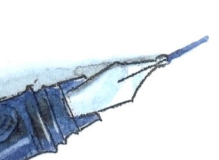

Shale Gas Shocks the Energy Portfolio

Natural gas is yet another fossil fuel resource that will continue making significant contribution to the world energy economy. The cleanest of all fossil-based fuels, natural gas is plentiful and flexible. It is increasingly used in the most efficient power generation technologies, such as Combined Cycle Gas Turbine (CCGT)[1] with conversion efficiencies[2] of about 60%. The reserves of conventional natural gas have grown by 36% over the past two decades and its production by 61%. Compared to the 2010 survey, the proved natural gas reserves have grown by 3% and production by 15%.

The exploration, development and transport of gas usually requires significant upfront[3] investment. Close coordination between investment in the gas and power infrastructure is necessary.

In its search for secure, sustainable and affordable supplies of energy, the world is turning its attention to unconventional energy resources. Shale gas is one of them. It has turned upside down the North American gas markets, and is making significant strides[4] in other regions. The emergence of shale gas as a potentially major energy source can have serious strategic implications for geopolitics and the energy industry. The most credible studies put the global shale gas resource endowment[5] at 456 tcm.[6] There are about 700 known shales worldwide in more than 150 basins. At present only a few of these shales have had properly assessed production potentials, most of those are in North America. The potential volumes of shale gas are enormous and this is likely to reshape significantly the gas markets and LNG markets worldwide.

Source: WEC: World Energy Resources (2013, Survey, Summary, p. 14-15)

M1 Excerpt from a report by the World Energy Council

① Sum up the text in German.

_____

_____

_____

_____

_____

_____

_____

_____

② Explain the sentence: 'The reserves of conventional natural gas have grown by 36 per cent over the past two decades and its production by 61 per cent.'

③ Comment on the further and increased use of natural gas worldwide.

 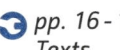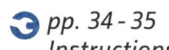
Energy Resources

Nuclear Energy – Friend or Foe?

Nuclear energy and the environment

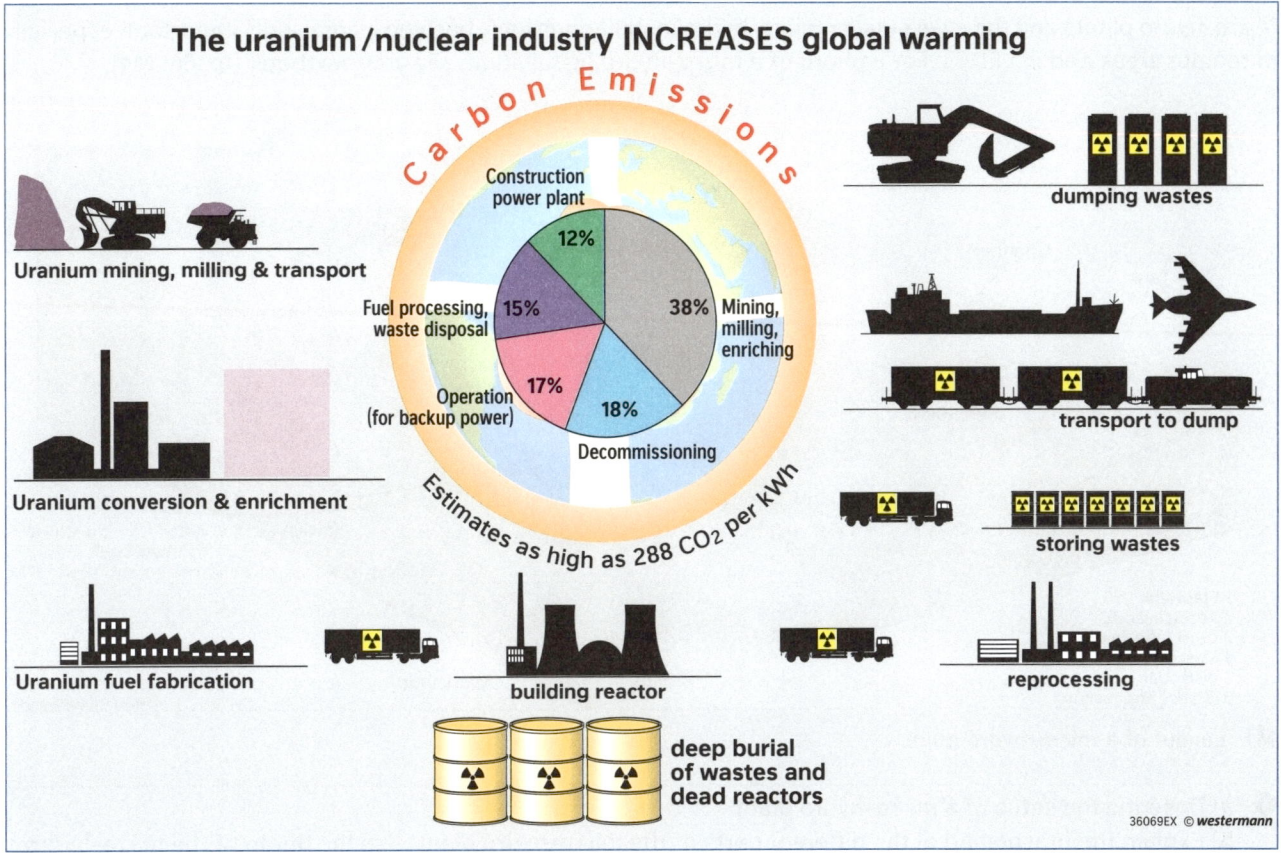

M1 After a poster from anti-nuclear protesters

1 Describe the claims made in the poster.

2 Research these claims.

Internet research for 'nuclear power' + 'fuel cycle' + 'greenhouse gas'

1.

_____

_____

2.

_____

_____

3.

_____

_____

3 Compare the greenhouse gas emissions of nuclear energy with that of other non-renewable fuels.

Hydropower – Electricity from Water?

Analysing micro-hydro installations

Micro-hydro plants and the even smaller micro-hydro installations have become increasingly important, especially in remote areas and in LEDCs. For a photo of a micro-hydro installation, see your textbook (›p. 66: **M4**).

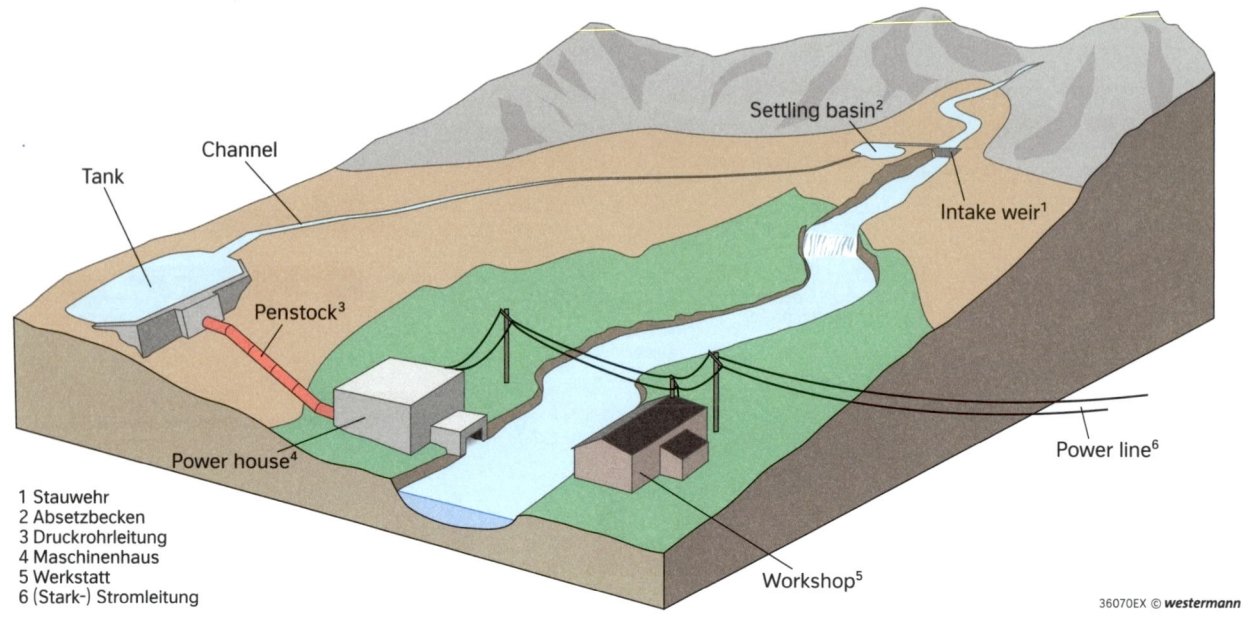

1 Stauwehr
2 Absetzbecken
3 Druckrohrleitung
4 Maschinenhaus
5 Werkstatt
6 (Stark-) Stromleitung

36070EX © *westermann*

M1 Layout of a micro-hydro plant

❶ a) Describe the setup of a micro-hydro plant.
   b) Explain the functioning of the different parts of the micro-hydro plant. Use the photo of the micro-hydro installation in your textbook (›p. 66: **M4**).

Structure	Function
Intake weir	
Settling basin	
Channel	
Tank	
Penstock	
Power house	
Workshop	
Power line	

❷ Compare micro-hydro plants with run-of-the river power stations.

_____

_____

_____

❸ Comment on the effect of micro-hydro plants on nearby communities in remote regions.

 100800-066, -108
schueler.diercke.de

 DE-110
www.diercke.com

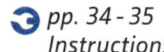 *pp. 34-35*
Instructions

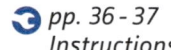 *pp. 36-37*
Instructions

Energy Resources

Bioenergy – Not just Firewood

Clean energy for LEDCs

ACE *(africancleanenergy.com)* is a company from Lesotho. It sells the ACE 1, a 'solar biomass cookstove', for approximately $100 per unit or similar.

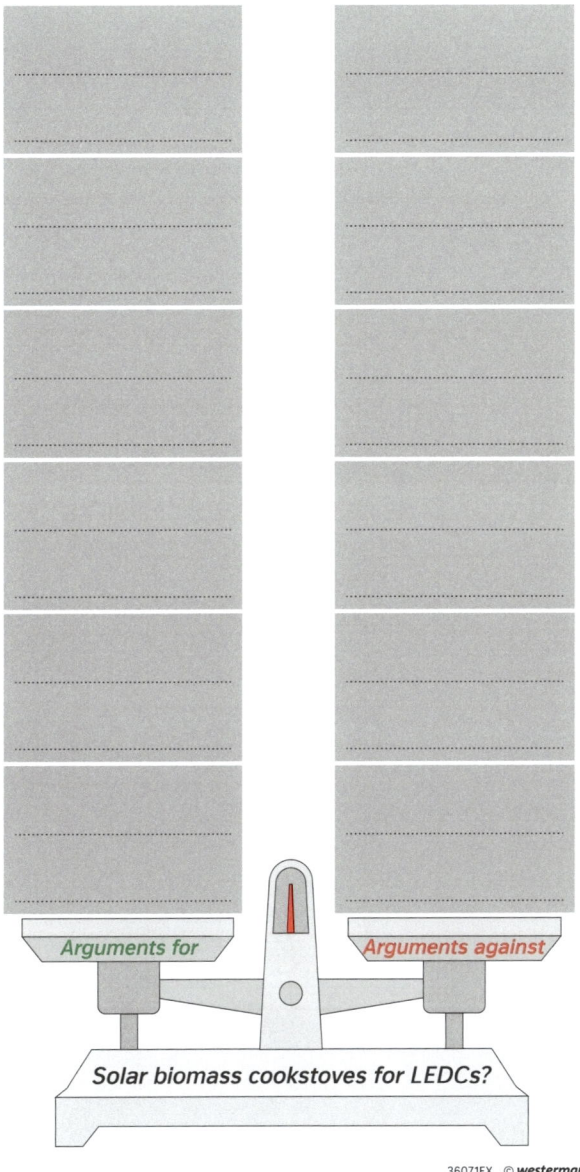

M1 Evaluation balance scale

❶ Describe the multiple uses of the cookstove (**M2**).

❷ a) List the arguments for and against the cookstove with the help of an evaluation balance scale (**M1**). Staple your arguments from the scales upwards, each in a box!
b) Discuss the importance of the arguments.

❸ Contrast the use of the cookstove to the traditional use of biomass in LEDCs (textbook ›p. 68: **M1**).

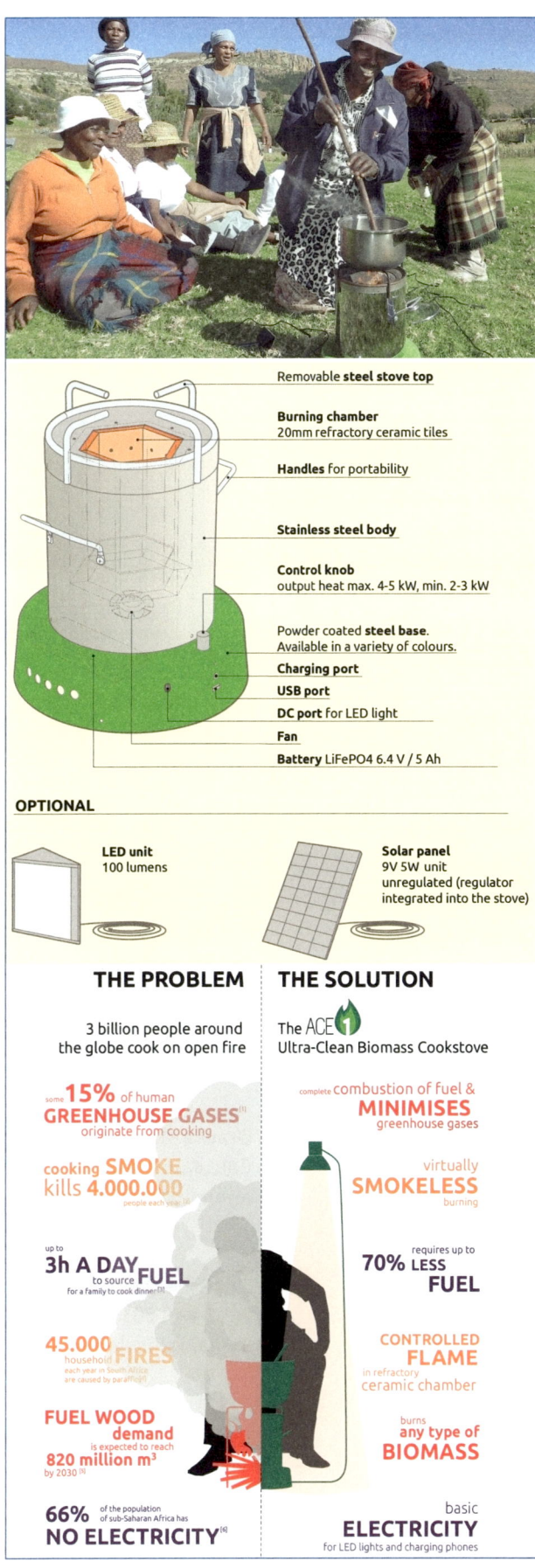

M2 From an advert for a solar biomass cookstove

Energy – Blown by the Wind

The rise of wind energy

Year	2005	2006	2007	2008	2009	2010	2011	2012	2013	2014	2015
Additions (GW)	12	15	20	27	38	39	41	45	36	52	63
Capacity (GW)	59	74	94	121	159	198	238	283	318	370	433
Growth rate (%)											

Source: REN21 Renewables 2016 Global Status Report

M1 Wind power, annual additions and global capacity (2005–2015)

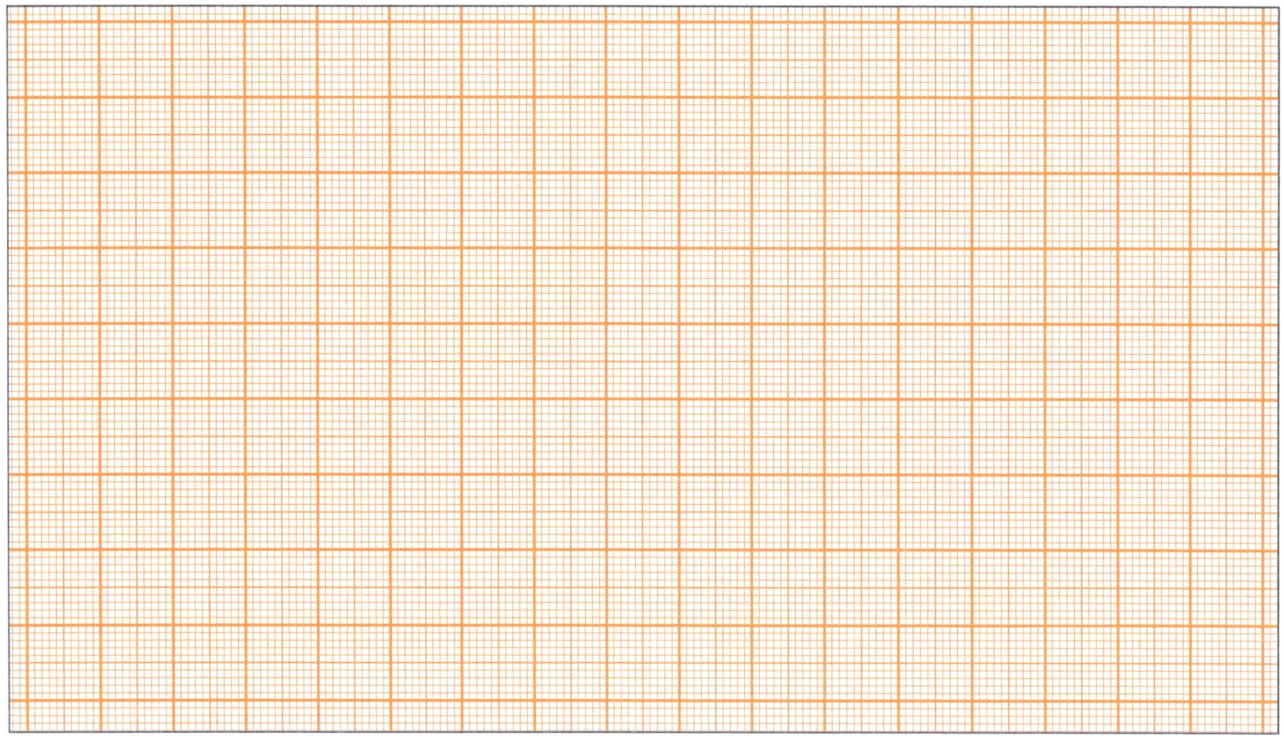

HELPFUL HINT

for TASK 1 (b):

· Calculation for 2006:
  15/59*100 = 25.4 %

1 a) Draw a stacked bar graph from the data given in **M1**.
   b) Calculate the growth rate of the worldwide wind power (i.e. the percentage of the annual additions to the capacity of the previous year) from 2005 to 2015 in **M1**.

2 a) Describe the development of global wind power as an energy source between 2005 and 2015.
   b) Explain this development.

3 Suggest locations for offshore wind parks in Europe. See textbook (›p. 70: **M2**) and an economic map of Europe for clues.

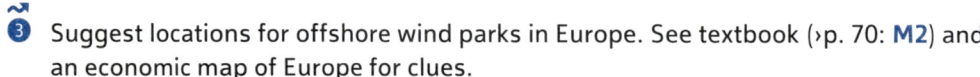

100800-066
schueler.diercke.de

DE-049
www.diercke.com

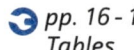
pp. 16 - 17
Tables

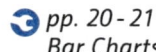
pp. 20 - 21
Bar Charts

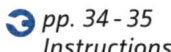
pp. 34 - 35
Instructions

Energy Resources

Solar Energy – Let the Sunshine in

Photovoltaics to the fore!

1 Describe the development of the regional distribution of the global capacity of photovoltaic solar power (**M1**). Write down the five most important observations.

1. _____

_____

2. _____

_____

3. _____

_____

4. _____

_____

5. _____

_____

2 a) Compare the solar potential (textbook ›p. 72: **M2**) with the countries using PV.
   b) Explain your results.

3 Prepare for a discussion (in German) about ways to increase the use of photovoltaic power in countries with high solar radiation like Egypt.

HELPFUL WORDS AND PHRASES
for TASK 2a:
- as, as compared with, as well as ...
- comparable, comparatively ...
- equal, identical, like, of little/no difference, resemble, same as ...

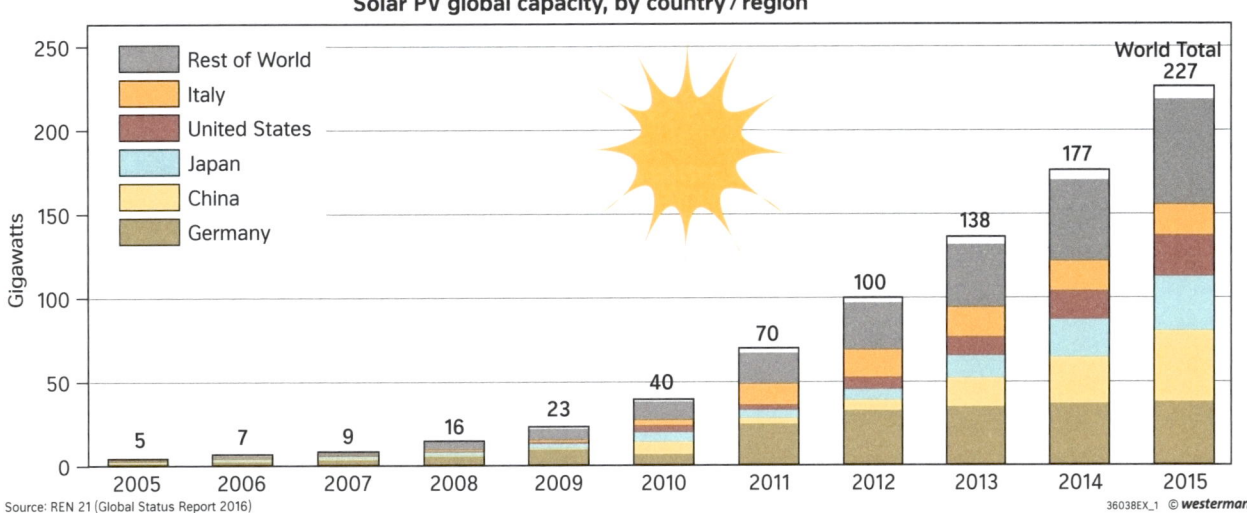

M1 Development of the solar photovoltaic global capacity

Other Renewable Energies

Tapping energy from the underground

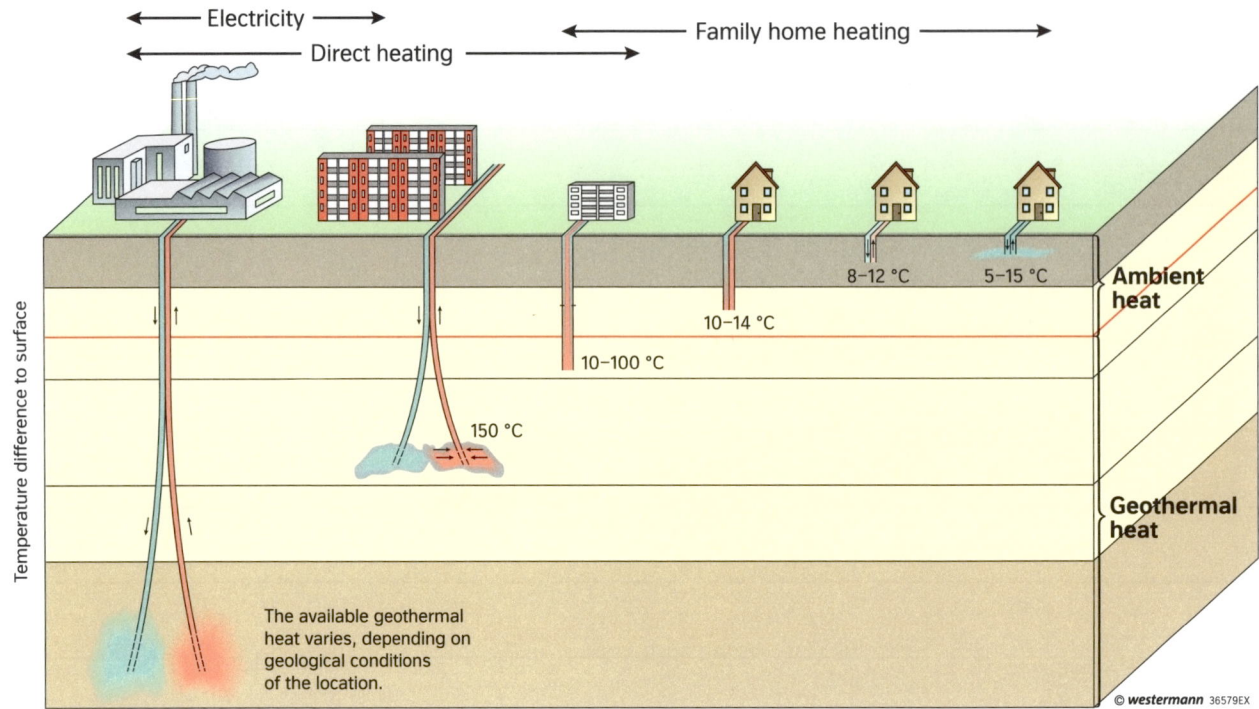

M1 Extracting underground heat

HELPFUL HINTS

for TASK 1:
- Use all the technical terms from M1 . Observe the arrows and the different colours of the underground pipes.

for TASK 3:
- Find a fitting title. You might add a photo.

❶ Explain the different uses of underground heat (**M1**).

❷ Research about an underground heat scheme in your area on the basis of the questionnaire below.

Location	
Energy source	
Depth	
Energy gained (which kind of energy, how much)	
Number of households supplied	
Remarks	

❸ Write a German newspaper article about it.

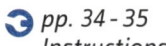

100800-068, -108 schueler.diercke.de • DE-049 www.diercke.com • *pp. 34 - 35 Instructions*

Energy Resources

World Energy – Challenges and Perspectives

Electricity is the energy of renewables

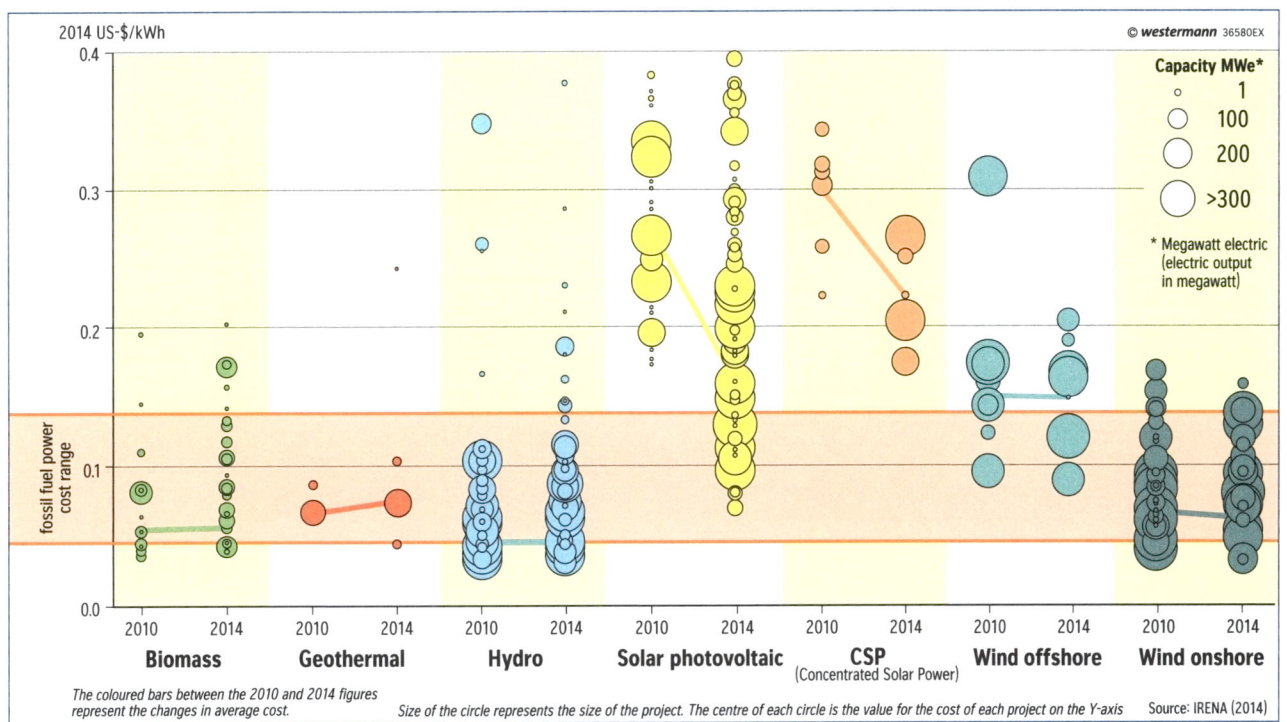

M1 Cost of electricity from newly installed renewable sources 2010 and 2014

❶ Describe the costs of renewable energy production for 2014 in the text below. Add the missing data and use the answer for biomass as template for the other sources.

The electricity production cost range produced by biomass was between _____ and _____ US cent

per kWh. It came from power stations with capacities from _____ to _____ MW, most of them being

smaller. The average production cost in 2014 was at around _____ US cent per kWh.

❷ Do a research to compare the costs for electricity from renewable energies to that of non-renewables.

_____

_____

_____

_____

_____

❸ Prepare for a discussion about the future production cost development based on **M1** and your knowledge about renewable energy sources and fossil energies.

pp. 36 - 37
Instructions

Changing Climate

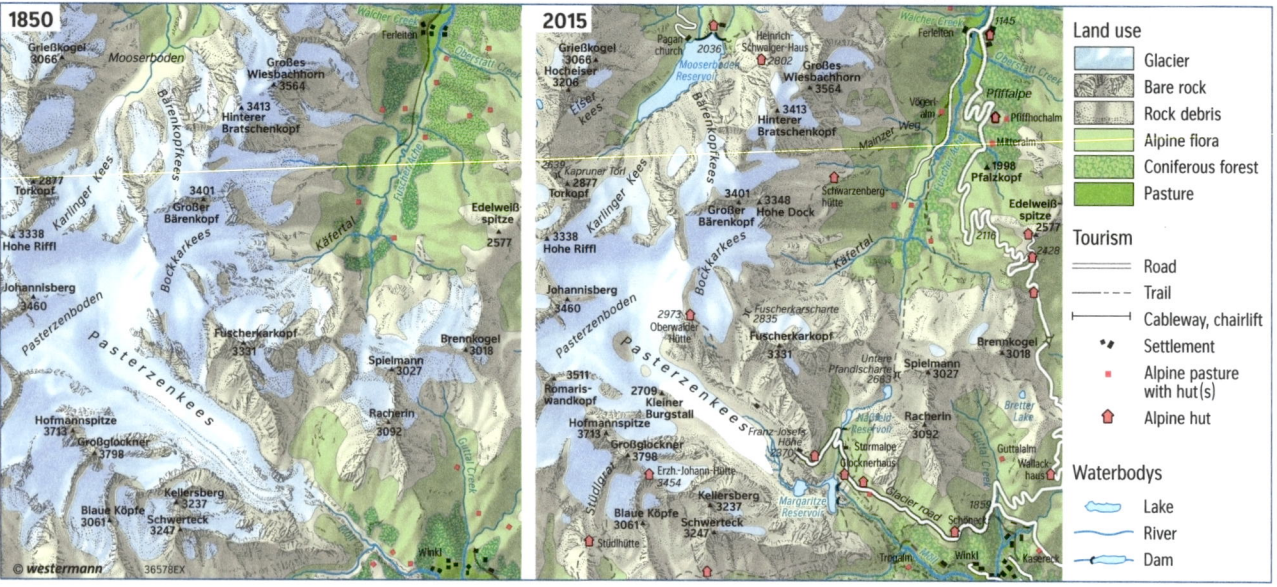

M1 Changing landscape near the Großglocknermassiv

1 a) Compare the maps in **M1** and write down main changes in the landscape.
b) Explain these changes.

_____

_____

_____

_____

_____

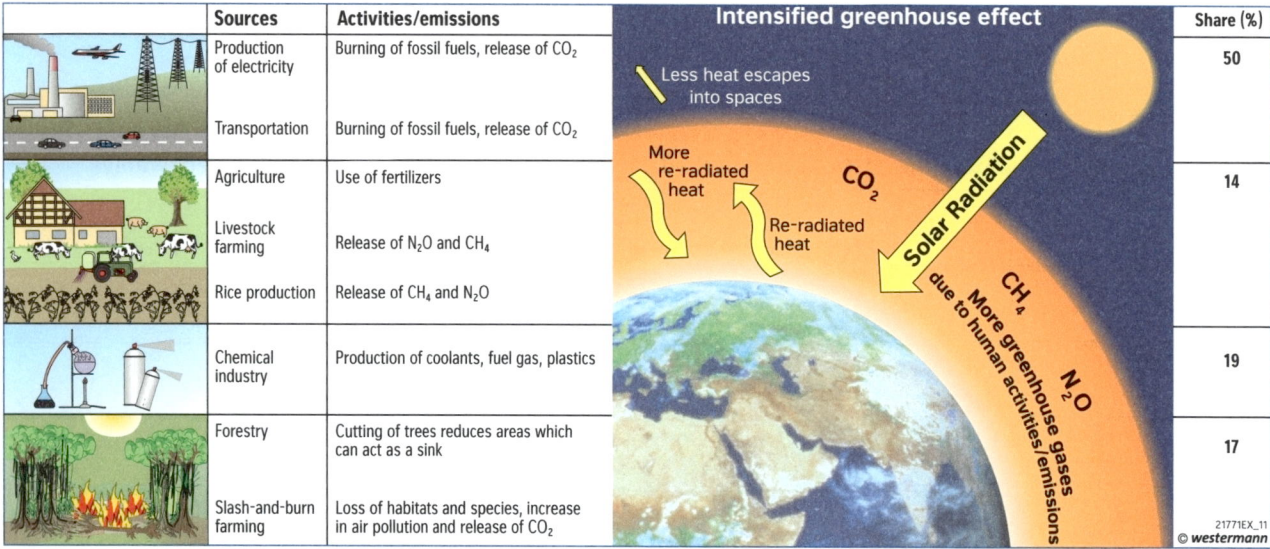

M2 Greenhouse gases

2 Choose one source of greenhouse gases (**M2**) and explain the emission in detail. Use the Internet.

3 Look for opportunities to reduce the emission of greenhouse gases.

100800-60-2, -250 schueler.diercke.de   DE-078, 198 www.diercke.com   **>** *pp. 10-11* Thematic Maps   **>** *pp. 36-37* Instructions

People Leave Their Carbon Footprint

1 a) True or false? Tick the correct boxes.

Structure	True	False
1. All living things contain the element carbon (C) in energy-rich chemical bindings.		
2. Plants absorb energy-poor carbon dioxide and turn it into energy-rich biomass.		
3. Since the beginning of the industrialisation, CO_2 emission to the atmosphere is much lower than CO_2 absorption.		
4. The total sum of all the greenhouse gas emissions make up the Carbon Footprint (CF).		
5. In societies with low living standards, plenty of greenhouse gases are produced.		
6. Rich countries are encouraged to support poor countries with energy-consuming technology and know-how.		

b) Rewrite the false statements from a) as true ones.

_____

_____

_____

_____

_____

_____

_____

'The most common way to reduce the carbon footprint of humans is to reduce, reuse, recycle, refuse.'

(Source: https://simple.wikipedia.org)

2 a) Explain the main idea of the statement above.
b) Give at least two examples for opportunities in daily life to act according to the statement.

to reduce: _____

to reuse: _____

to recycle: _____

to refuse: _____

Examples: _____

_____

_____

Soil Degradation – Losing Arable Land

1 Form sentences by combining the appropriate heads and tails from the table below.

Structure	Tails	Match
1. Soil degradation is a general term ...	A ... and has negative impacts on the environment.	*1. –*
2. Raindrops and surface water flows ...	B ... can also be caused by wind.	*2. –*
3. Irrigation without drainage often results in ...	C ... which has been accelerated by human activities.	*3. –*
4. By water erosion the soil is physically disrupted ...	D ... reduce pore spaces in the soil.	*4. –*
5. It reduces the productivity of soils ...	E ...for a number of different unfavourable processes on the Earth's surface.	*5. –*
6. Removal of topsoil material ...	F ... has been moderately to severely degraded within the last 60 years.	*6. –*
7. Soil erosion is a natural process ...	G ... to increase the fertility.	*7. –*
8. The use of heavy machinery and the trampling by livestock ...	H ... and the previously used land is dissected.	*8. –*
9. Estimates show that more than ten per cent of the Earth's land area ...	I ... soil degradation caused by the process of salinization.	*9. –*
10. Many farmers add chemical substances to the soil ...	J ... can erode the soil and lead to the formation of rills.	*10. –*

2 Describe the process of soil degradation presented in the pictures **M1** and **M2** below.

_____

_____

_____

_____

_____

M1 Example of soil degradation

M2 Example of soil degradation

 100800-257 schueler.diercke.de  DE-198 www.diercke.com ↻ *pp. 10-11 Thematic Maps* ↻ *pp. 36-37 Instructions*

Environment – Global Change

Fresh Water – A Vital Resource

Water conservation

1 Explain the following statement: *'Water has to be carefully managed during every part of the water cycle.'*

_____

_____

_____

_____

_____

_____

_____

_____

Condensation

Precipitation

Rain

Snow

Evaporation

Surface Runoff

Groundwater

© *westermann* 36577EX

M1 Water cycle process

Here is a list of things you and your family can do:

Action	Already done	Will do	Will not do
Buy organic products.			
Minimise wastewater.			
Avoid using chemical pesticides and biocides in your own garden, and use fertiliser sparingly.			
Always clean your car at the car wash.			
Avoid land sealing or use permeable surfacing materials.			
Ensure that rainwater seepage meets the best available technology.			
Have your sewage tanks and private sewer connections checked for leaks and upgraded where necessary.			
Have your own wells and geothermal installations installed by a specialist.			
Avoid the use of salt in winter.			
Dispose of batteries and accumulators properly.			

2 a) Add one more action to complete the checklist.
b) Explain why the actions may contribute to water conservation. (Choose at least three examples.)
c) Discuss your results in class.

 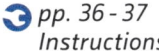

Threatened Oceans

Plastics in the oceans

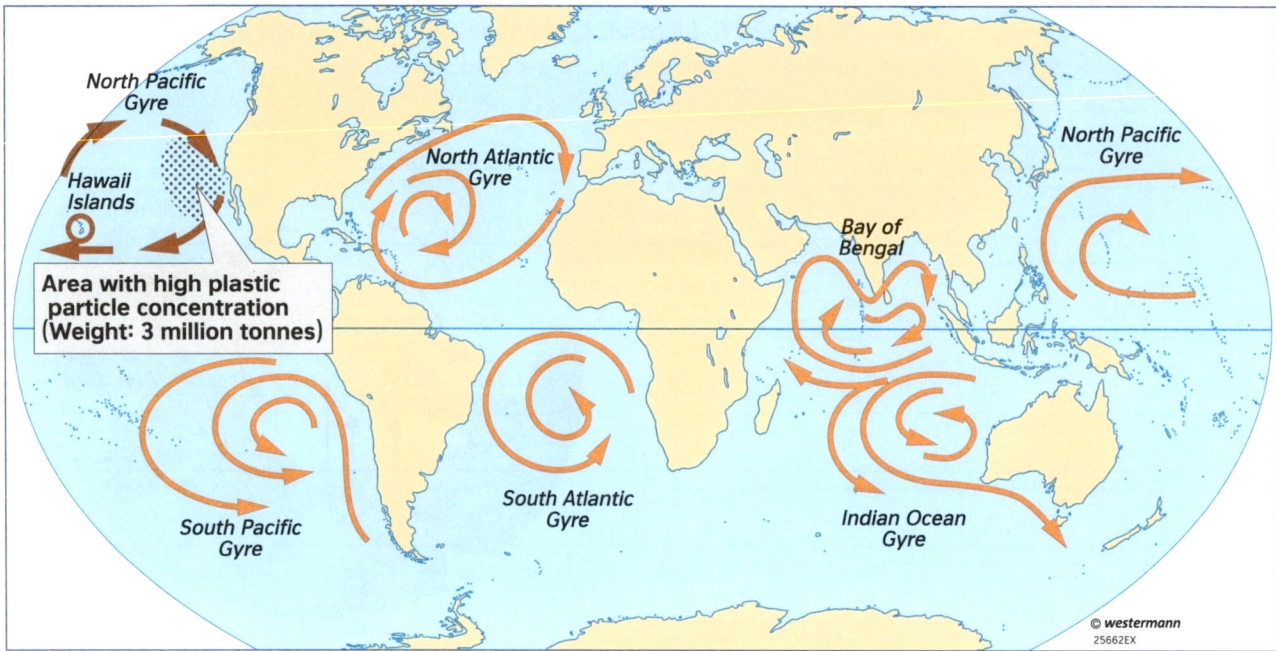

M1 Garbage patches in the oceans

> Ocean currents are movements of ocean water. They are continuous and directed and they flow on the ocean's surface and in its depths, both, locally and globally.

> The name 'garbage patch' is wrong, since there is no island of trash forming in the middle of the ocean. Much of the debris found here is small bits of floating plastic. It is not easily seen from a boat.

1 Name ocean currents corresponding with the garbage patches.

_____

_____

_____

2 a) Find out about sources of plastics in oceans.

b) Comment on the consequences of plastics pollution in oceans.

Plastics in oceans

at the surface of oceans   deposited at the sea-bottom   deposited at shores

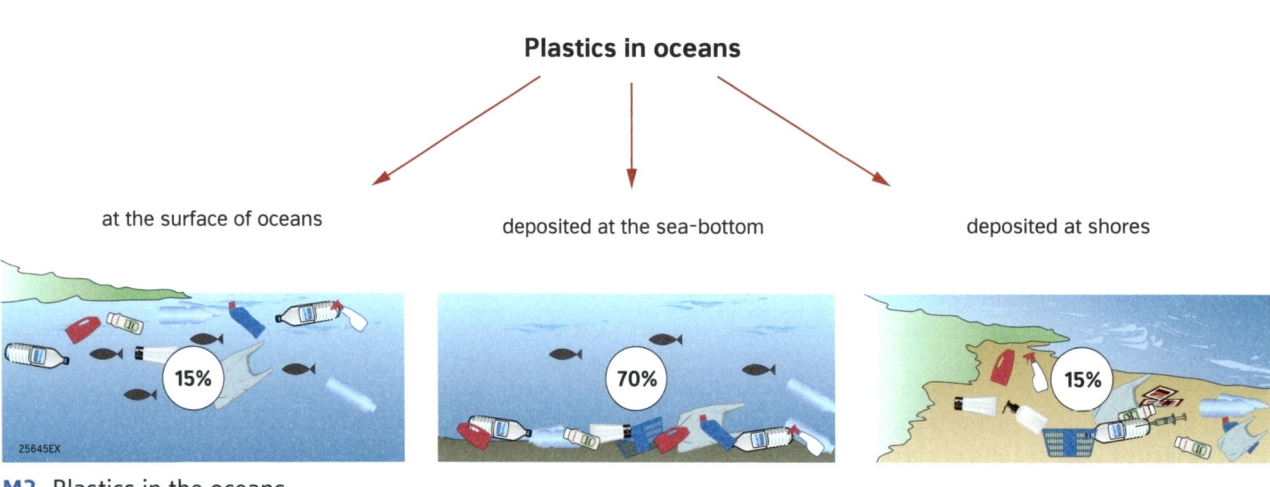

M2 Plastics in the oceans

Environment – Global Change

 100800-251, 263
schueler.diercke.de

↪ pp. 34-35
Instructions

The Ecological Footprint

How 'green' are you?

"We're trying to discourage carrier bag use."

M1 Cartoon

❶ Analyse the cartoon **M1**. Write a short summary about your findings.

_____

_____

_____

_____

❷ Explain the following key terms in German.

Biocapacity:

_____

Ecological footprint:

_____

Ecological overshoot:

_____

Ecological deficit/reserve:

_____

❸ Calculate your own ecological footprint using the Internet.

 www.greencred.me

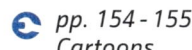 *pp. 154 - 155*
Cartoons   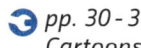 *pp. 30 - 31*
Cartoons

How to make money by planting trees

In the Mount Elgon landscape in Eastern Uganda [...], a community co-operative carbon offset[1] scheme, managed under (the) Trees for Global Benefit programme (TGB), [...] encourages small-scale farmers to adopt tree planting as a livelihood strategy supported by income from the sale of carbon sequestration[2] credits.[3]* TGB started in 2003 with 33 farmers, and has grown to include more than 4,600 farmers covering 4,887 hectares, with carbon trading now worth US $ 1.2 million annually. [...]

As one of the initial steps, poor communities have started engaging in new livelihood activities including beekeeping and producing non-timber forest products, which can be developed as important sources of cash and non-cash incomes. Communities and landowners have benefited from practical training on simple and affordable small-scale irrigation techniques. A number of households have adopted these techniques, as evidenced by sustained crop yields, even during long dry spells. Erosion protection and management measures (e.g. constructing contour trenches and stabilising them with grass and shrubs) have also been promoted[4] to enable landowners maximise crop production. [...]

Farmers with less than the required minimum of land for tree planting can now join their land together with other farmers, and apply as a group to access carbon benefits. TGB has also put in place mechanisms to provide benefits for non-participants by involving them in tree nursery[5] operations, accessing free firewood from tree pruning[6] and helping in the sale of tree products (e.g. fruits, timber, charcoal and firewood) harvested from TGB farms. In addition, 10 per cent of income from the sale of carbon credits is used to capitalise[7] a fund that supports communitywide projects. Using an agroforestry approach, TGB has identified suitable tree species for intercropping[8] within banana and coffee farming to provide shade. This is improving farmers' crop productivity in their plantations. Farmers have also been able to sell sequestered carbon credits from these agroforestry trees.

Source: IUCN Forest Brief, No.11 (08/2016)

*Carbon sequestration credit = Money paid to the farmers for each tonne of carbon their trees bind (sequestrate) by photosynthesis. It is divided in five instalments[9] as follows: 30 per cent of farmers total computed payment after planting 50 per cent of expected trees in the year farmer begins planting (year 0),followed by 20 per cent payment in the following year 1 after planting all the expected trees as in the carbon sale contract. Thereafter, farmers are paid another 20 per cent if the surviving trees are 85 per cent in year 3, then 10 per cent and 20 per cent payments if the average diameter at breast height of the trees in year 5 and 10 is 10cm and 20cm respectively. No further payments are given to farmers.

HELPFUL WORDS

for M1:

1 – Reduzierung von Kohlenstoffemission

2 – Kohlenstoffbindung in Biomasse

3 – Guthaben

4 – fördern

5 – Baumschule

6 – Beschneidung

7 – mit Geld versorgen

8 – Mischkultur

9 – Rate

M1 From a report by the International Union for Conservation of Nature and Natural Resources

1 Sum up the text in German.

_____

_____

_____

_____

2 Explain which Sustainable Development Goals are targeted by this TGB programme.

_____

_____

_____

3 Compare this programme with the principle of sustainable forestry.

Sustainable Development

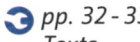 *pp. 32-33* Texts   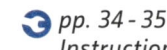 *pp. 34-35* Instructions   *pp. 36-37* Instructions

John Miller was born in 1932. He is living in the rural area in Oklahoma and he is one of the many people who suffered from the Dust Bowl in the 1930s.

❶ Find the questions to John Miller's answers.

Q1: Hello John. You and your family experienced the Dust Bowl in the 1930s. What exactly happened then?

John Miller: *'The dust storms blew away everything we possessed. We lost huge areas of fertile land and our livestock. It was a difficult and desperate time. Since we were pretty poor, we had to stay in Oklahoma and had to wait for better times.'*

Q2: _____
John Miller: *'When the drought and dust storms showed no signs of letting up, many other people, who were rich enough, escaped. About 200,000 people abandoned their land and left the Plains. They packed everything they had into their cars and trucks and headed west towards California.'*

Q3: _____
John Miller: *'Arriving in California, the migrants were faced with a life almost as difficult as the one they had left. Many California farms were large corporate farms. They were more modernized than those of the southern plains, and the crops were unfamiliar. The fields of wheat were replaced by crops of fruit, nuts and vegetables. As a result, many migrants gave up farming.'*

Q4: _____
John Miller: *'I heard that a lot of these migrants worked in the San Joaquin Valley, picking grapes and cotton. They were paid by the quantity of fruit and cotton picked with earnings ranging from 75 cents to $ 1.25 a day.'*

Q5: _____
John Miller: *'They built little shacks – without plumbing and electricity – near larger cities in shacktowns called Little Oklahomas or Okievilles. Polluted water and a lack of waste facilities led to outbreaks of severe diseases such as malaria for example.'*

Q6: _____
John Miller: *'Over the years, they replaced their shacks with real houses, sending their children to local schools and becoming part of the communities. However, they continued to face discrimination when looking for jobs and they were called 'Okies' and 'Arkies' by the locals regardless of where they had come from.'*

Q7: _____
John Miller: *'The situation in the Plains got worse. But we stayed. We just had to. My family and I hoped that every year would become a better one as the previous one. Unfortunately nothing changed until 1939. In 1935, when I was 13 years old, Congress even declared soil erosion 'a national menace'. Therefore, new farming techniques such as strip cropping and contour farming were advocated.'*

Q8: _____
John Miller: *'Here were many farmers who had lot of trouble adapting to these new techniques. Moreover, the use of costly machines, which required technical skills, was needed. The government itself waxed and waned in terms of its enthusiam for supporting them.'*

Q9: _____
John Miller: *'Additionally to new farming techniques, which had been suggested by the government in 1935, two years later, in 1937, President Franklin Roosevelt launched the Shelterbelt Project. It was about the large-scale planting of trees across the Great Plains, functioning as windbreaks. Rows of these trees can still be seen throughout western Oklahoma and the Panhandle today.'*

❷ Write an article about the Dust Bowl in the 1930s in German or English.

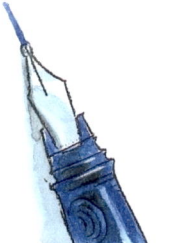

Mumbai (India) – Sustainability of Plastic Recycling

Recycling plastics in Dharavi

Details	Plastic recycling
Plastic handled per month (in tonnes)	13-18
Cost of recycling per kg (in US-$)	0.30
Selling price per kg (in US-$)	1.05
Annual turnover per year (in US-$)	15,000 - 37,500
Number of permanent workers	2-8
Number of casual workers	8-10 (when required)
Monthly income for owner (in US-$)	155-390
Taxes paid	None

M1 Economies of an average plastic waste recycling enterprise in Dharavi

❶ Answer - in whole sentences - the following questions with the help of **M1** and **M2**.
   a) How much plastic is recycled per year in an average plastic recycling enterprise in Dharavi?
   b) How many taxes do the owners and workers in the recycling industry pay?
   c) Where do the workers in the plastic recycling industry mainly come from?
   d) Why wouldn't you like to work in a plastic recycling job in Dharavi?

❷ a) Make up four more questions from the information given in **M1** and **M2**.
   b) Discuss the answers in class.

Average age (in years)	20-25
Literacy level	Primary education
State of origin/birth (mainly)	Uttar Pradesh, Bihar
Number of daily working hours (male / female)	8-10 / 6-8
Number of workdays per week	6
Wages per day (male/female, in US-$)	3.00-4.50 / 2.30
Savings per month (in US-$)	46.50-62.00
Actual work done (male / female)	All / Plastic waste sorting
Chief expenditure	Health
Duration of employment per year (in months)	8-9
Personnel protective equipment	None
Social security	None
Taxes paid	None

M2 Socio-economic details of workers in the plastic recycling industry in Dharavi

 100800-182
schueler.diercke.de
▶ *pp. 36 - 37*
Instructions

(side tab) Sustainable Develpment

Indonesia – Sustainable Population Development

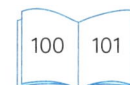

1 Draw a combined bar and line graph showing the development of Indonesia's total population and growth rate between 1965 and 2015 (textbook ›p. 100: **M2**).

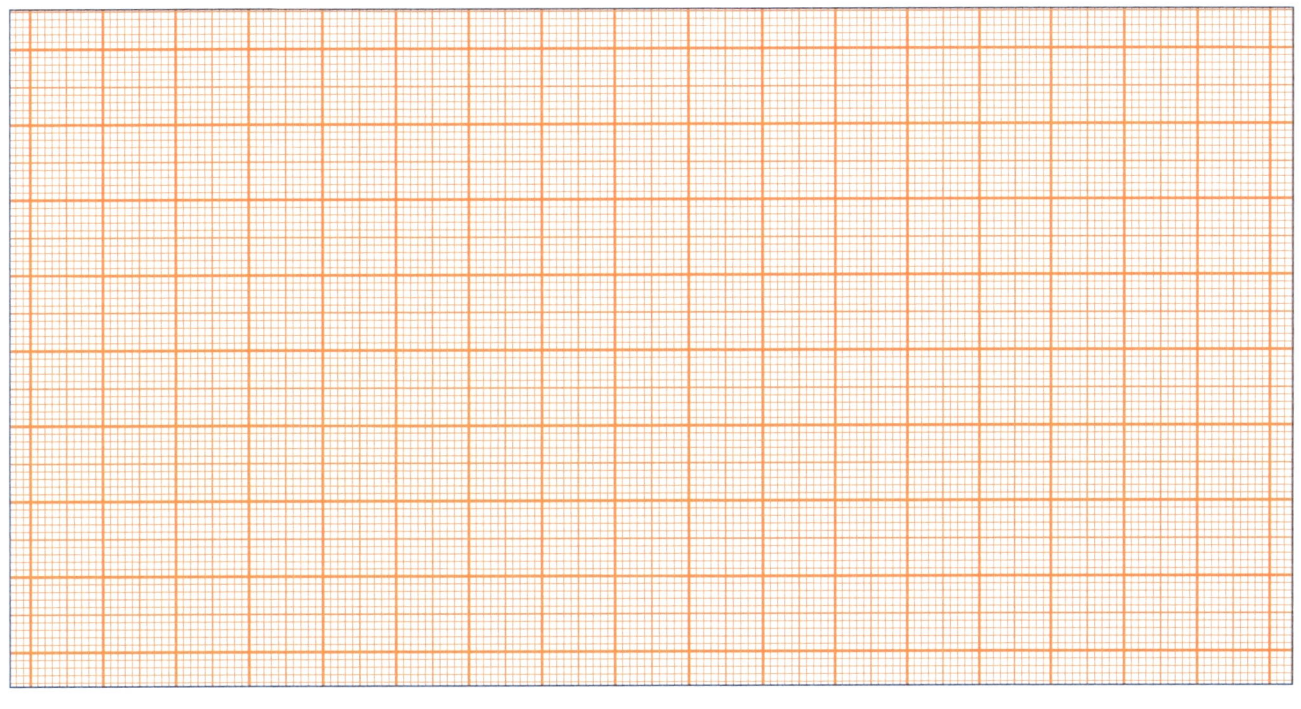

2 Make three statements about the data shown in your graph.

_____

_____

_____

_____

3 Comment on Sukarno's statement (textbook ›p. 100) with regard to the data shown in your graph.

_____

_____

_____

_____

_____

_____

 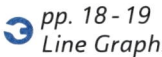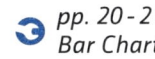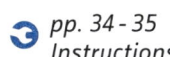

Think Globally – Act Locally

What can YOU do?

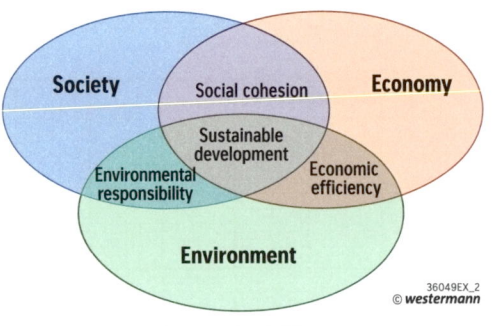

36049EX_2
© **westermann**

M1 Aspects of sustainability

There are Local Agenda 21 projects in cities and local communities which you can join or contribute to.

Furthermore, there are various things you can do at home in order to act in a sustainable way.

1 Fill in the boxes with key words in English or German.

Your sustainable behaviour In what way do/could you act in a sustainable way on your way to school and back home/during the lesson/ in the breaks/on class trips ...?	Sustainabilty in your local community In what way do/could your community act in a sustainable way in terms of nature conservation/ traffic/water management/social welfare ...?
What I already do:	*What is already done:*
What could I do:	*What could be done:*

Sustainable behaviour of your parents In what way do/could your parents act in a sustainable way on their way to work and back home in their leisure time ...?	Your school environment/school building In what way is your school area sustainable with regard to waste arisings and disposal/paper consumption/energy production and demand ...?
What they already do:	*What is already done:*
What could they do:	*What could be done:*

Sustainable Develpment

46

The European Union (EU) and Me

Travellin' Europe

After your graduation, you are planning on taking a trip through at least five European countries with some friends.

1 Mark the cities/places you would like to visit in the map and draw in the route you would like to take.

M1 Travel map

2 a) Note down facts about your travel route that you find interesting (distances, points of interest). Use your atlas.

b) Explain which advantages you will experience during your trip thanks to the existence of the EU.

_____

_____

_____

_____

_____

_____

 100800-084
schueler.diercke.de
 DE-039
www.diercke.com
↻ *pp. 34 - 35*
Instructions

47

The European Union and the World

The EU compared with other powers

1 Compare the EU to the USA, and the BRICS-states by taking a closer look at the area size, population numbers and the GDP. Use your textbook (›p. 108: **M1**, ›p. 109: **M3**).

_____

_____

_____

_____

_____

_____

_____

2 Write down four statements about the situation of the EU concerning international trade (**M1**).

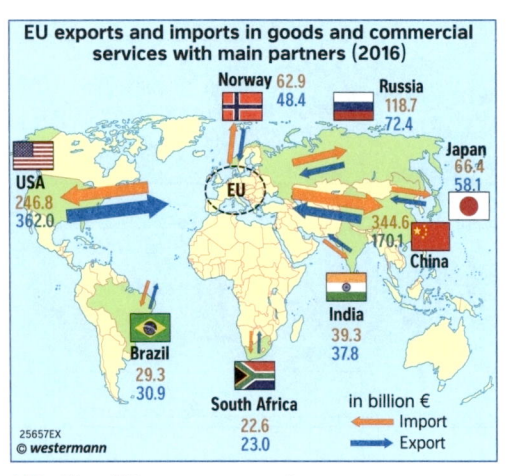

M1 The EU – an economic power

1. _____

_____

2. _____

_____

3. _____

_____

4. _____

_____

3 Comment on the statement from the textbook '_The EU has achieved a strong position by acting together with one voice on the global stage rather than with 28 separate trade strategies._' Use your own words.

_____

_____

_____

_____

_____

Europe Changes

Regional Disparities in the EU

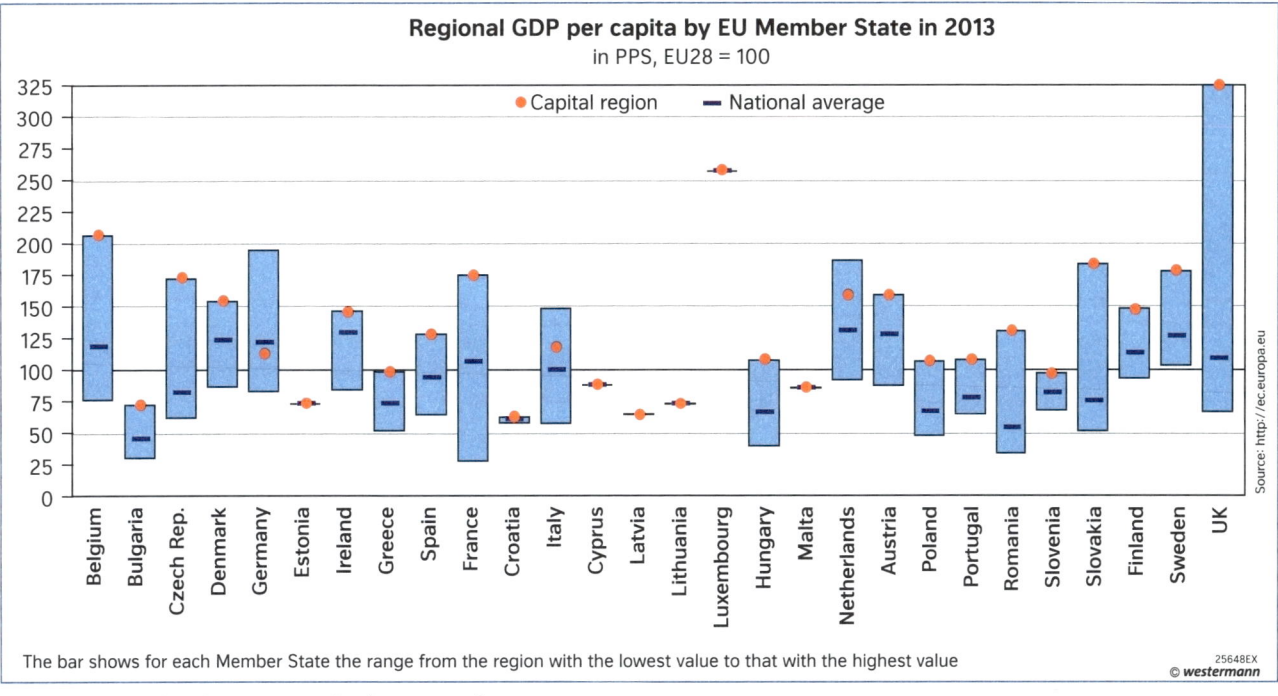

M1 The EU – the GDP per capita in comparison

❶ List six EU member states which are characterised by high regional disparities concerning their GDP per capita (**M1**).

1. _____   4. _____

2. _____   5. _____

3. _____   6. _____

❷ a) List countries with a high as well as a low national average concerning their GDP per capita.

High national average	Low national average

b) Explain these differences by taking a closer look at the economy, the employment structure as well as the unemployment rate of the countries. Use your atlas.

_____

_____

_____

_____

The Regional Policy of the EU

How Europe supports Saxony-Anhalt (ERDF 2014-2020)

Erwartete Wirkungen

(1) Die meisten Mittel (30 Prozent) sind für die Stärkung von Forschung und Entwicklung und die Verbesserung der angewandten Forschung in Sachsen-Anhalt [...] vorgesehen. Dementsprechend wird erwartet, dass die immer noch unzureichenden Ausgaben für F&E in der von kleinen und mittleren Unternehmen (KMU) dominierten Wirtschaft steigen. Dementsprechend kann die gut ausgebaute öffentliche Forschungs-Infrastruktur besser für ein wissensbasiertes Wirtschaftswachstum genutzt werden. In diesem Zusammenhang werden 355 F&E-Projekte und 163 Kooperationsprojekte zwischen Forschungsinstituten und Unternehmen umgesetzt. Es wird erwartet, dass etwa 80 Mio. EUR privater Mittel von Unternehmen für Forschungs- und Innovationsprojekte mobilisiert werden.

(2) Die Steigerung der Wettbewerbsfähigkeit von KMU in Sachsen-Anhalt erfolgt [...] durch die Förderung von mehr Produktivität, die Markteinführung neuer, innovativer Produkte und die Entwicklung einer wirtschaftlich relevanten Infrastruktur. Es wird erwartet, dass durch die produktiven Investitionen 3775 neue Arbeitsplätze in 1842 geförderten Unternehmen entstehen.

(3) Die Umstellung auf eine CO_2-arme Wirtschaft wird durch Investitionen unterstützt, welche die Energieeffizienz in öffentlichen Gebäuden und Unternehmen erhöhen. Daneben werden umweltfreundliche, emissionsarme Beförderungsarten unterstützt. Mit diesen Maßnahmen sollen die Treibhausgasemissionen 2023 auf etwa 32 t CO_2-Äquivalent reduziert werden.

(4) Im Hinblick auf die vermehrten extremen Wetterbedingungen durch den Klimawandel ist die Risikoprävention in Sachsen Anhalt von großer Wichtigkeit. Die EFRE-Förderung für Risikoprävention dient vor allem dem Überschwemmungsschutz. Schätzungsweise 75 000 Personen profitieren von den durch den EFRE kofinanziert Maßnahmen zum Schutz vor Überschwemmung.

(5) 5 % der Mittel werden verwendet, um die Umweltprobleme in Stadtgebieten anzugehen. Dazu gehören auch die Bewahrung und der Ausbau des Kulturerbes. Dementsprechend ist eines der Ziele die Aufwertung von 102 ha des öffentlichen Raums in Stadtgebieten. Darüber hinaus fließt 1 % der Mittel in Investitionen im Rahmen lokaler, von der örtlichen Bevölkerung betriebener Entwicklungsstrategien.

Source: http://ec.europa.eu (2017)

M1 Excerpt of the programme description for ERDF Saxony-Anhalt (2014-2020)

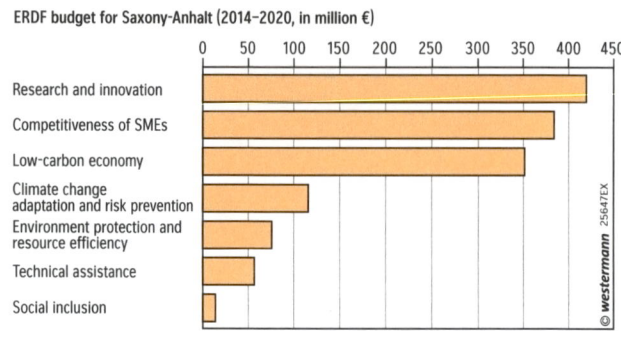

ERDF budget for Saxony-Anhalt (2014–2020, in million €)

M2 ERDF budget for Saxony-Anhalt

❶ Explain the strategy used in Saxony-Anhalt to implement each goal (textbook ›p. 113) in a statement.

1. _____

_____

_____

_____

_____

2. _____

_____

_____

_____

3. _____

_____

_____

4. _____

_____

5. _____

_____

_____

⮕ pp. 20-21 *Bar Charts*   ⮕ pp. 34-37 *Instructions*

Europe Changes

The Common Agricultural Policy of the EU

1 a) Romania and Bulgaria are the most agrarian-oriented countries within the EU. Find out which kind of agriculture is used in these countries. Use your atlas.

Romania:

_____

_____

Bulgaria:

_____

_____

b) Discuss whether the distribution of CAP allocations is reasonable from their point of view.

2 a) Decide whether these statements are in favour of or against the CAP. Mark them with '+' or '–'.

The CAP leads to overproduction, forming mountains of surplus produce which are either destroyed or dumped on developing nations, undermining the livelihoods of farmers there. ◯

Increasingly, the CAP is used to protect the rural environment. Farmers get more if they sign up to agro-environment commitments – using fewer chemicals; leaving boundaries uncultivated; maintaining ponds, trees and hedges and protecting wildlife. ◯

Europe has the world's best food and CAP promotes quality and diversity.
Abolishing the CAP would put such delights under threat and put Europe on a diet of bland processed foods churned out by US-style factory farms. ◯

The idea that the CAP protects small farmers is a myth. 80 per cent of CAP aid goes to just 20 per cent of the farms. The most subsidies are handed to the landed gentry, environment-destroying mega-farms and vast agro-industrial conglomerates. ◯

The CAP gives Europe food security. Without it, we would be dangerously dependent on fluctuating imports. ◯

Farmers represent 3 per cent of the EU's population. They generate roughly 6 per cent of the Union's GDP.
Yet they receive 30 per cent of the EU's total budget through CAP handouts. ◯

Source: www.debatingeurope.eu

b) List the main arguments below using your own words.

In favour of the CAP	Against the CAP

Connecting Europe – Case Examples

The Fehmarn Belt Fixed Link

❶ a) Locate the cities of Hamburg, Kiel, Lübeck, Copenhagen, Malmö, Goteborg as well as the islands of Fehmarn and Lolland and mark them in the map (**M1**).

M1 Map

b) Mark ferry routes from Germany and Denmark to Sweden in the map. Use your atlas.

❷ a) Calculate the travel times of a lorry (70 km/h) from Hamburg to Gothenborg when choosing the land route (incl. bridges) vs. the ferry.
Annotations:
- *The ferry takes 14.5 hours from Kiel to Gothenborg.*
- *Choosing the ferry means you have to check in at least 30 minutes before departure.*
- *Keep in mind that a lorry driver has to take a 45-minute-break after 4.5 hours.*

b) Compare these times to the travel time of a lorry from Hamburg when the new Fehmarn Belt Fixed Link is finished.

Land route: *Ferry:*   *Fehmarn Belt Fixed Link:*

❸ Evaluate the building of the Fehmarn Belt Fixed Link on the basis of the concept of sustainability (**M2**).

M2 The concept of sustainability

100800-104
schueler.diercke.de

DE-054
www.diercke.com

pp. 04 - 05
Atlas

The European Car Industry Moves East

Example – Slovakia

Slovakia stays strong in automotive

The automotive industry is one of the pillars of Slovakia's economy, bringing investment, employment and innovations with the planned Jaguar Land Rover plant in Nitra as the latest example. [...]

Slovakia is already home to three carmakers, Volkswagen Slovakia, PSA Peugeot Citroën Slovakia and Kia Motors Slovakia. Over the past 20 years, car production increased from 2,952 vehicles in 1993 to more than 970,000 in 2014. The latter figure, equalling 178 cars per 1,000 citizens, has made Slovakia the biggest per capita producer in the world. "There are several viewpoints by which to define the importance of the automotive industry for Slovakia," Juraj Sinay, president of the Automotive Industry Association of the Slovak Republic (ZAP), told The Slovak Spectator.

The car industry employs 80,000 people but when also subcontractors and other related sectors and services are included, the automotive industry gives jobs to more than 200,000 people. The automotive industry generates 13% of the gross domestic product (GDP) and makes up 43% of the total industrial production in Slovakia.

"The structure of production technologies in [automotive] companies in Slovakia includes the most modern solutions nearing alternatives of a digital company, which was also one of the reasons why another important investor ponders investment in Slovakia," said Sinay. "But these are only some of the factors being cited by our foreign partners as added value."

The importance of the automotive industry for the economy of Slovakia is gradually increasing [...]. Production of transport vehicles, which for the first time in 2010 represented more than 20% of total industrial sales, has gradually increased its share of total up to 28.7% in the first half of 2015.

"Taken together with all the subcontractors, who are classified in other industries, the total share of the overall automotive cluster for the economy of Slovakia is even higher," Vaňo told The Slovak Spectator.

[...] While Slovakia's carmaking industry manufactures about 6,000 electric and hybrid cars annually, less than 300 such cars are currently on the country's roads. The cabinet sees the development of electric mobility as a chance for Slovakia to improve its environment as well as put an impetus on innovations and Research & Development and thus it adopted on September 9, 2015, the Strategy of Support of Electromobility. [...]

Source: https://spectator.sme.sk (28 Dec 2015)

M1 Excerpt from a magazine report

1 a) Mark all the effects in the text **M1** the founding of car plants has already had on the country of Slovakia.
b) Write them down in your own words.

_____

_____

_____

_____

_____

_____

_____

_____

_____

2 Describe what is done in Slovakia's automotive industry to preserve this positive development.

_____

_____

_____

_____

_____

_____

_____

_____

_____

_____

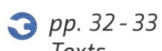 *pp. 32 - 33*
Texts

The EU – Quo Vadis?

A video analysis

1 How does the EU work?
   a) Select a video presented on **http://www.bbc.com/news/world-europe-23488006** (**M1**)
   and analyse it with the help of page 69 in this workbook.
   b) Present your findings in class.

2 What future for Europe? Select one politician and analyse the video presented on:
http://www.euronews.com/2017/03/24/what-future-for-europe (**M2**). Use page 69.
(Note that you can also find the text of the interviews on the website for help.)

Opinion of: _____

Opinion about the EU's future (summary, conclusion): _____

_____

_____

_____

_____

_____

_____

_____

_____

_____

_____

_____

_____

_____

_____

3 Research more videos about the European Union on the Internet:

_____

_____

_____

Europe Changes

Germany – A Leading World Economy

1 Fill in the gaps with the help of your textbook.

At the end of the 19ᵗʰ century most people worked in _____ . Many workers

were needed during the age of industrialisation because it was _____ to produce things.

Nowadays, the agricultural and industrial production are less labour-intensive due to

_____ , _____ , and _____ .

Germany's reputation as a leading economy is mainly based on the _____ of high

quality goods. The total value of export goods accounted for _____ in year 2015, whereas

the _____ amounted to 948 billion Euros.

Germany's most important kinds of _____ are vehicles, machinery, chemical

products and electronics. Important kinds of import goods are _____ ,

_____ , and _____ .

The three economic sectors contribute to Germany's GDP in different shares. _____ (____%)

contributes to a very small part to Germany's GDP. Almost one third of the GDP is generated in the

_____ (30 %). The tertiary sector is responsible for even ____% of Germany's GDP.

2 a) True or false? Work with your textbook (›p. 124: **M2**). Tick the correct boxes.

Statement	True	False
1. German employees today mainly work in the secondary sector.		
2. At the beginning of the 20ᵗʰ century more than 40 per cent of the people in Germany worked in the primary sector.		
3. The tertiary sector has always been very important for the German economy.		
4. The primary sector today offers only a few jobs for the German people.		
5. At the end of the 1960s, German people mainly worked in the industry.		

b) Correct the false statments in German or English.

_____

_____

_____

Demographic Change

1 Complete the diagram by writing the phrases in the correct boxes.

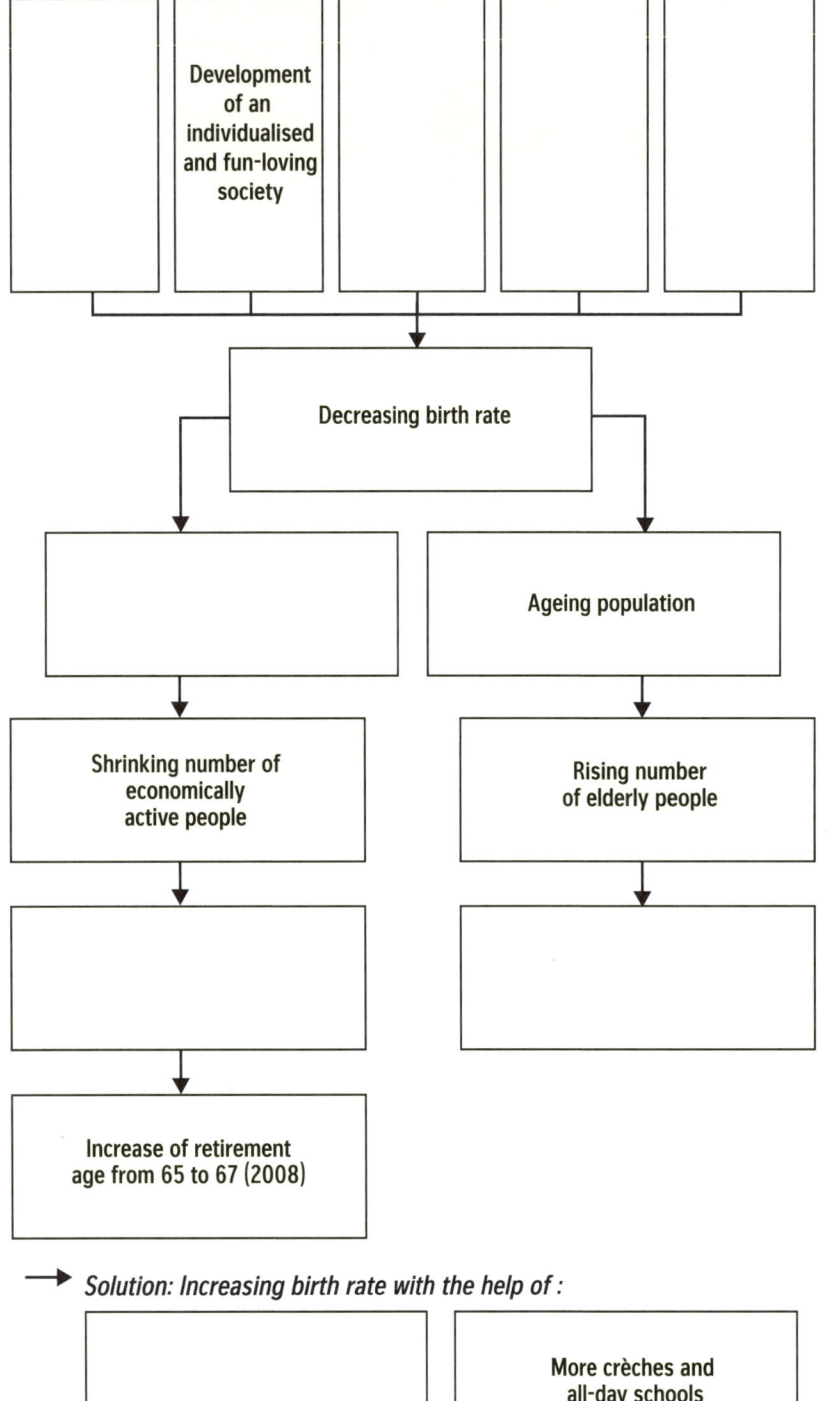

- *Aspiration of self-fulfilment and flexibility*

- *More health care*

- *Long-term care of the elderly and sheltered housing is needed*

- *Incentives (cash bonus for parents)*

- *Launch of the contraceptive pill in the 1960s*

- *Shrinking population*

- *Children are not considered as labour force and social security*

- *Achievement of a far-reaching women's equality in working life*

(Diagram boxes:)

Development of an individualised and fun-loving society

Decreasing birth rate

Ageing population

Shrinking number of economically active people

Rising number of elderly people

Increase of retirement age from 65 to 67 (2008)

→ *Solution: Increasing birth rate with the help of :*

More crèches and all-day schools

25666EX
© *westermann*

2 Prepare a talk about the demographic change in German or English by using the diagram.

 100800-080, -081
schueler.diercke.de

 DE-042
www.diercke.com

pp. 28 - 29
Flow Charts

Germany in a Changing World

A Land of Contrasts – Regional Disparities in Germany

1 Analyse how the maps **M1-M3** in your textbook (›p. 128) can be related to each other.

_____

_____

_____

_____

_____

_____

_____

_____

2 a) Give examples of regions that are highly affected or slightly affected by population ageing and depopulation (**M1**).

_____

_____

_____

_____

_____

_____

b) Note down areas where the provision of public/private services is below or well below average (**M1**).

_____

_____

_____

_____

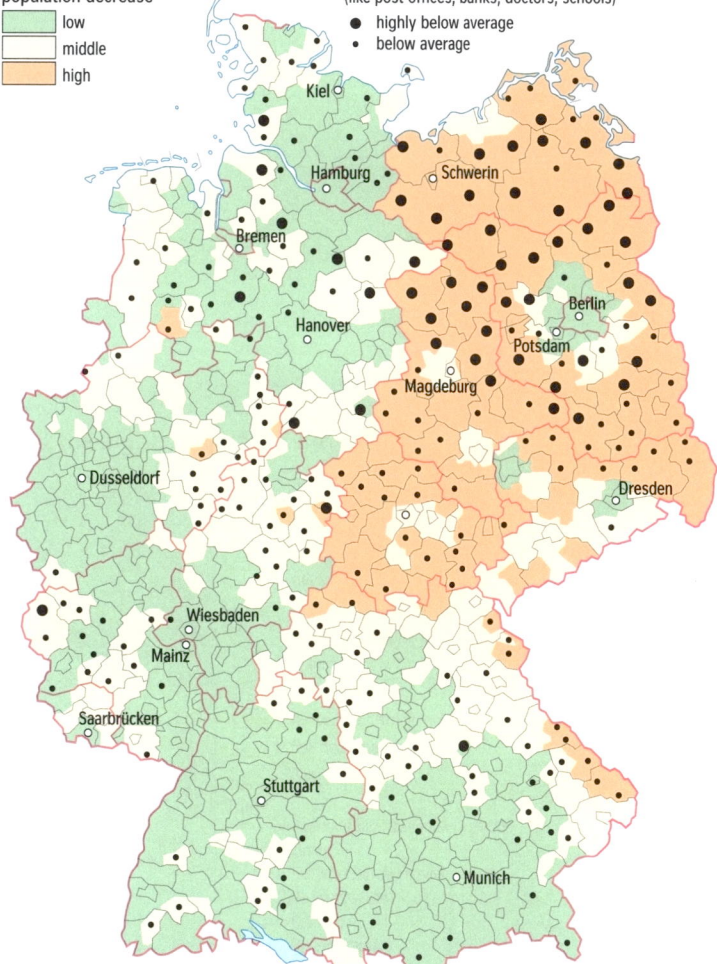

M1 Demographic change and infrastructure

Regional Migration in Germany

Problems in rural Germany

Half Empty – The Slow, Painful Demise[1] of Rural Germany

A massive exodus[2] is causing cities across Germany to swell while draining rural areas of people, money and life. While funds are needed elsewhere, should more be done to save dying communities?

[In the northern Bavarian town of Nordhalben 85 out of the 820 houses are empty. The town had 3,000 inhabitants not too long ago, but now there are only 1,900.] "Nobody lives there anymore," mayor Daum says, pointing to a mintgreen single-family house. The Edeka grocery store closed its doors for good last year, and no trains have passed through the town since 1994. [...]

Most state contributions to municipalities[3] depend on their population figures. But since people are moving away from Nordhalben, it has had to borrow 3.5 million € just to make ends meet.[4] [...] "If we were a company, we'd be a classic case of insolvency", Daum says. [...] Even his daughter has moved away to Munich, because that's where the jobs are. [...]

Granted[5], young people have always been attracted to big cities - and, with them, many of the companies that fight bitter battles to attract the brightest minds.

Under these circumstances rural areas watch their finances dry up. [...] The Berlin Institute for Population and Development has concluded that, for "financial and environmental reasons," there is no sense in maintaining the infrastructure of sparsely populated[6] regions. According to this scenario, small, isolated villages without links to transport arteries would eventually be abandoned. [...] Similar situations can be found all across rural Germany. Since there aren't enough local jobs, people are forced to commute[7]. Since they buy their groceries on the way home from work, the village stores are eventually forced to close. When clubs and associations start to dissolve, solidarity disappears. Then people move away, and a vicious cycle[8] is set in motion. [...]

[Some] areas have gone out looking to attract foreigners. For example, representatives from the towns of Einbeck, Uslar and Dassel, in Lower Saxony, presented their municipalities at a fair in Utrecht, Netherlands, as attractive retirement destinations, stressing the low real-estate prices, the proximity to low mountain ranges and the area's relative immunity to the effects of climate change.

Source: www.spiegel.de (12 May 2012, abridged)

M1 Excerpt from a newspapers article

1 Draw the vicious cycle referred to in the text. Use the phrases from the wordbag.

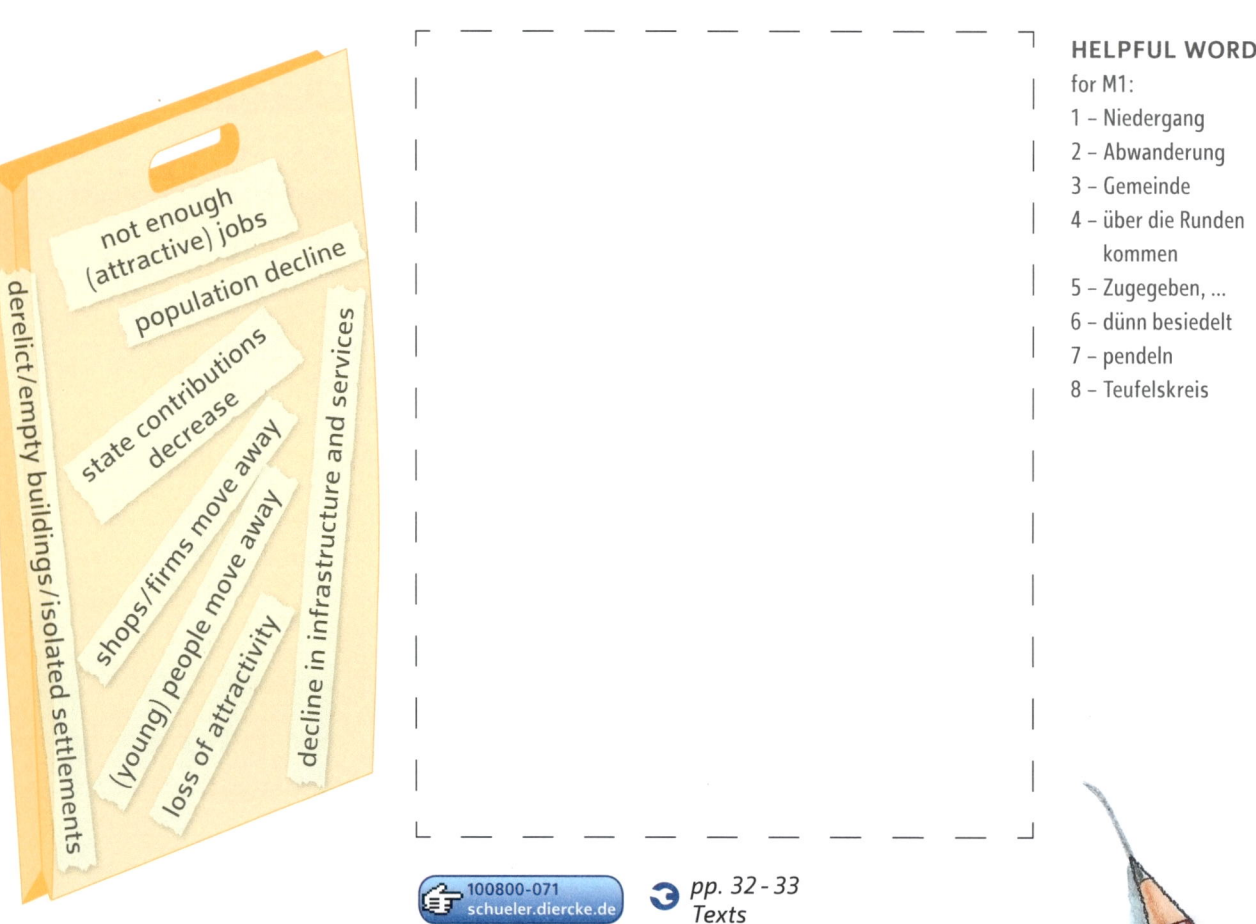

HELPFUL WORDS
for M1:
1 – Niedergang
2 – Abwanderung
3 – Gemeinde
4 – über die Runden kommen
5 – Zugegeben, ...
6 – dünn besiedelt
7 – pendeln
8 – Teufelskreis

Wordbag phrases: not enough (attractive) jobs · population decline · state contributions decrease · shops/firms move away · (young) people move away · decline in infrastructure and services · loss of attractivity · derelict/empty buildings/isolated settlements

100800-071 schueler.diercke.de

pp. 32-33
Texts

Germany in a Changing World

Migration to and from Germany

Guest workers in Germany

Country	1965	1973
Italy	372,000	450,000
Greece	187,000	250,000
Spain	183,000	190,000
Turkey	133,000	605,000
Portugal	14,000	85,000
Yugoslavia	64,000	535,000
Others	264,000	480,000
Total	1,217,000	2,595,000

M1 Guest workers in Germany according to nationalities

❶ Turn **M1** into two pie charts.

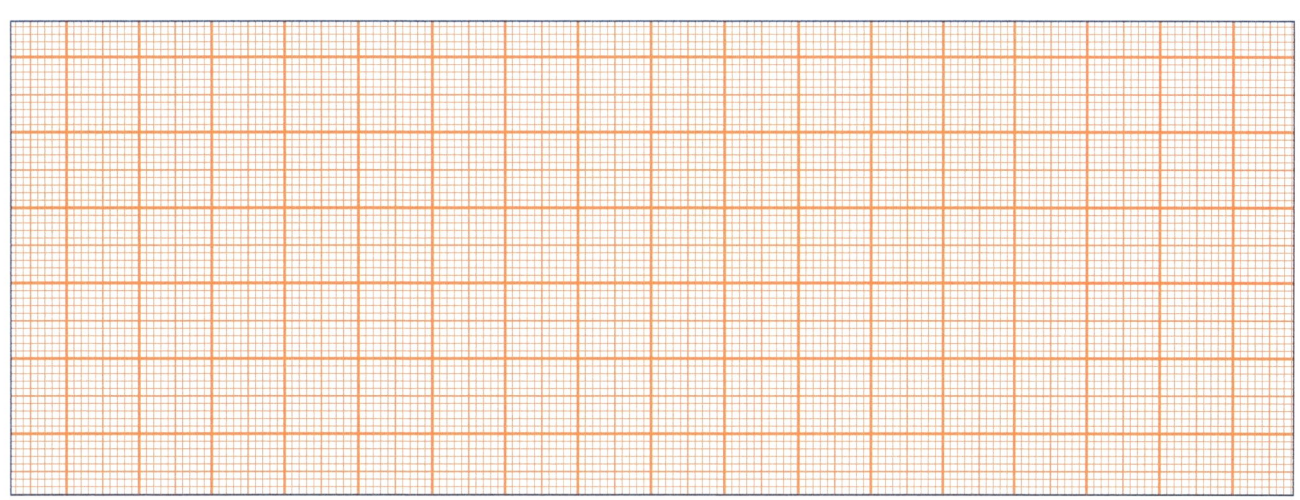

❷ Describe the data shown in your pie charts.

_____

_____

_____

_____

❸ Compare the data of your pie charts with that of ›p. 133: **M5** in your textbook.

_____

_____

_____

_____

pp. 20-21 Thematic Maps   pp. 36-37 Instructions

A Bright Future? – Germany's Energy Transition

A German village without fossil fuels

Erläuterung des Modells Bioenergiedorf

1 Fahrsilo: Im Fahrsilo lagert das Substrat für die Biogasanlage.

2 Dosierer: Durch den Dosierer wird das Substrat zerkleinert und gemischt. Dadurch werden die enthaltenen Nährstoffe den Bakterien im Fermenter besser zugänglich gemacht. Portionsweise wird dieses Gemisch dem Fermenter zugeführt.

3 Fermenter: Im Fermenter wird die zugeführte Biomasse zu Biogas vergoren.

4 Gas-Aufbereitung: Mit einem speziellen Verfahren wird hier das Rohbiogas zu Biomethan (Bioerdgas) veredelt.

5 Gärprodukte-Lager: Sobald das Biogas nahezu vollständig aus dem Substrat entwichen ist, bleiben die Gärrückstände im wasser- und gasdichten Lagerbehälter zurück. Die Gärrückstände dienen als hochwertiger organischer Dünger.

6 Blockheizkraftwerk (BHKW): Hier wird das im Gasspeicher zwischengelagerte Biogas verstromt. Das BHKW besteht aus einem mit Biogas betriebenen Verbrennungsmotor, der einen Generator zur Stromerzeugung antreibt. Der Strom wird anschließend in das Stromnetz eingespeist. Die entstehende Wärme beheizt die Biogas-Fermenter und viele Gebäude über das Nahwärmenetz.

7 Trafostation: Hier wird der Strom aus den erneuerbaren Energien Biogas, Holz, Wind und Photovoltaik in das öffentliche Netz eingespeist.

8 Holzheizkraftwerk: Das Holzheizkraftwerk erzeugt Wärme und Strom aus Holz.

9 Biogas- und Stromtankstelle: Auf der linken Seite des Dioramas am Gemeindehaus steht die Erneuerbare-Strom-Tankstelle. Sie dient als Lademöglichkeit für Elektrofahrzeuge. Auf der rechten Seite befindet sich u. a. die Biogastankstelle „Drive green on biofuels". Hier können Kraftfahrzeuge auch Biomethan tanken.

10 Windkraft-Anlage

11 Photovoltaik-Anlage

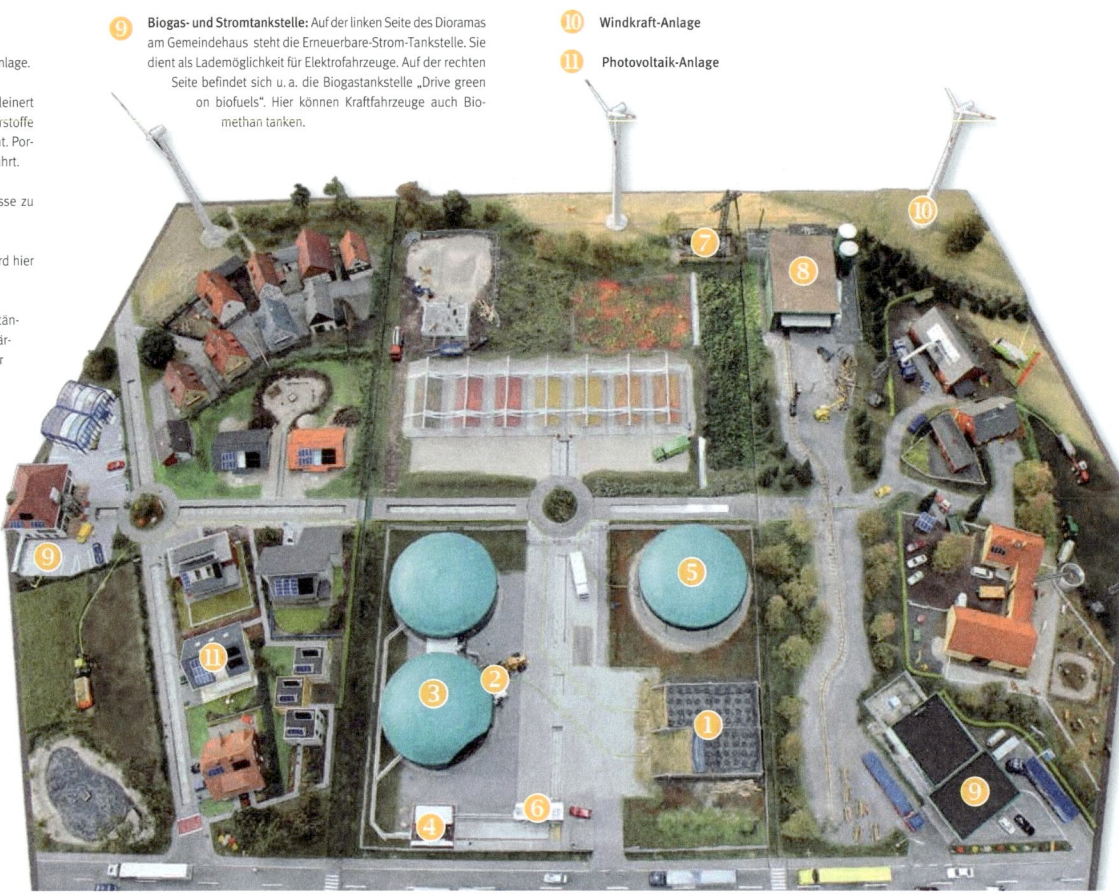

M1 Model of a bioenergy village

Germany in a Changing World

HELPFUL WORDS
for M1 and TASK 1:
1 – movable silo
2 – dosing device
3 – digester
4 – gas processing
5 – fermentation residue storage tank
6 – decentrally combined heat and power station
7 – transformer station
8 – wood-fired thermal power station
9 – biogas and electricity filling station
10 – wind turbine
11 – photovoltaic panel

1 Describe the energy production in the model bioenergy village.

2 Complete the diagram about the inputs and outputs of the model village.

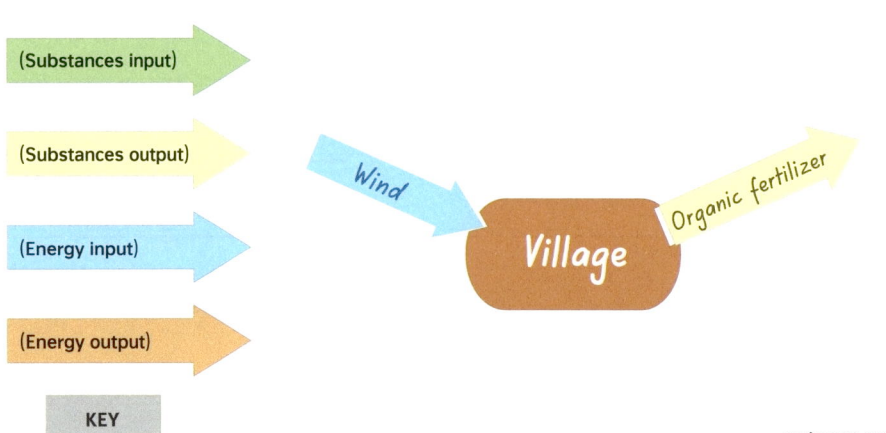

westermann 25661EX

3 Compare the model with the six aims of the German energy transition programme (see textbook ›p. 134) in your exercise book.

4 Prepare for a discussion in your exercise book about the consequences if more German villages were to be transformed into bioenergy villages.

  100800-068 schueler.diercke.de ➔ *pp. 36-37 Instructions*

Structural Changes in Agriculture

M1 Agriculture in Germany in the 1950s

During recent decades, agriculture in Germany and elsewhere in the world has undergone significant changes. These can be observed in many different aspects related to agriculture.

1 Find categories that are important when comparing agriculture in Germany in the past and today. Use the pictures and your textbook.

Category	Changes (key words)
Farm size	

2 Compare agriculture in the past and today.

_____

_____

_____

_____

_____

_____

_____

HELPFUL WORDS
for TASK 2:
- In contrast (to) ...
- Not only ... but also
- Compared to/with
  ... increases/decreases
- In comparison ...
- To sum up ...
- In conclusion ...
- However ...
- Whereas/Unlike/ While
- On the one / on the
  other hand ...

pp. 12-13 Photographs pp. 36-37 Instructions

Meat Production South of Oldenburg

Environmental problems

Niedersachsen hat ein dickes Mist-und Gülleproblem

Hannover – Kühe, Schweine, Hühner, Puten, Schafe - in Niedersachsen werden viele Millionen Nutztiere gehalten. Damit fallen jährlich rund 47 Millionen Tonnen Gülle und Mist an, die vor allem im Bezirk Weser-Ems für Probleme sorgen. Die in den Kreisen Cloppenburg, Vechta und Emsland konzentrierte Tierhaltung verfügt nicht über genügend Flächen, um allen Mist als Dünger auf die Felder zu bringen. Fast 66 000 Hektar mehr wären dafür nötig. Um Überdüngung zu vermeiden, werden jährlich rund 15 Millionen Tonnen an andere Betriebe oder in andere Regionen und Bundesländer abgegeben. 26 Millionen Tonnen können die Landwirte auf eigenen Feldern verwenden, sechs Millionen werden in Biogasanlagen in Energie umgesetzt.

Angesichts zu hoher Nitratwerte in Niedersachsens Grundwasser will Landwirtschaftsminister Christian Meyer (Grüne) sich für bundesweit strikte Düngeregeln stark machen. Im Vergleich zum letzten Bericht ist die Menge von 47 auf 47,6 Millionen Tonnen jährlich gestiegen. Für die in Teilen Niedersachsens schlechte Grundwasserqualität wird unter anderem eine Überdüngung durch die Landwirtschaft verantwortlich gemacht. [...]

Wie der Bund für Umwelt und Naturschutz (BUND) mitteilte, habe vor allem die Menge an Hühnertrockenkot weiter zugenommen. "Wir brauchen eine Abkehr von der Massentierhaltung mit ihren verheerenden Folgen für Natur und Umwelt", sagte der BUND-Landwirtschaftsreferent Tilman Uhlenhaut. Ein Gülle-Tourismus mit dem Transport in Ackerbauregionen, wo der Mist als Dünger begehrt ist, könne keine Lösung auf Dauer sein. "Bei rund 100 000 Lkw-Fahrten, die für den Transport notwendig sind, ist es sehr schwer zu kontrollieren, ob Gülle und Gärreste tatsächlich immer ordnungsgemäß abgegeben werden oder nicht doch auf überdüngten Feldern um die Ecke entsorgt werden."

Wie der Landesbauernverband in Hannover mitteilte, seien sich die Viehhalter der Düngeproblematik bewusst und arbeiteten bereits an einer Verbesserung der Situation. Aus dem Nordwesten Niedersachsens mit seiner intensiven Viehhaltung solle Dünger verstärkt in Ackerbauregionen geschaffen werden. Der Aufbau der dafür nötigen Infrastruktur wie etwa Lagerräume benötige eine gewisse Zeit, sagte Verbandssprecherin Gabi von der Brelie.

Source: www.abendblatt.de (17 Mar 2015)

M1 Excerpt from a newspapers article

1 Take different colours and mark
   a) characteristics of meat production in Lower Saxony.
   b) impacts of intensive livestock farming.
   c) solutions that are suggested.

2 Make a flow chart showing reasons and consequences of intensive livestock farming in Lower Saxony:

3 Prepare an interview between the farming minister of agriculture and a representative of the BUND discussing the issue of manure production.

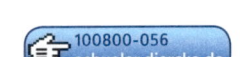

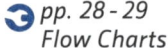 *pp. 28 - 29*
Flow Charts

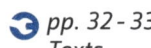 *pp. 32 - 33*
Texts

Germany in a Changing World

Rise and Fall of the German Coal Industry

1 Note four true statements about the economic structure of the Ruhr area in 1960 (**M1**).

1. _____

_____

_____

_____

2. _____

_____

_____

_____

3. _____

_____

_____

_____

4. _____

_____

_____

_____

2 Write four true statements about the economic structure of the Ruhr area today (**M2**).

1. _____

_____

_____

_____

2. _____

_____

_____

_____

3. _____

_____

_____

_____

4. _____

_____

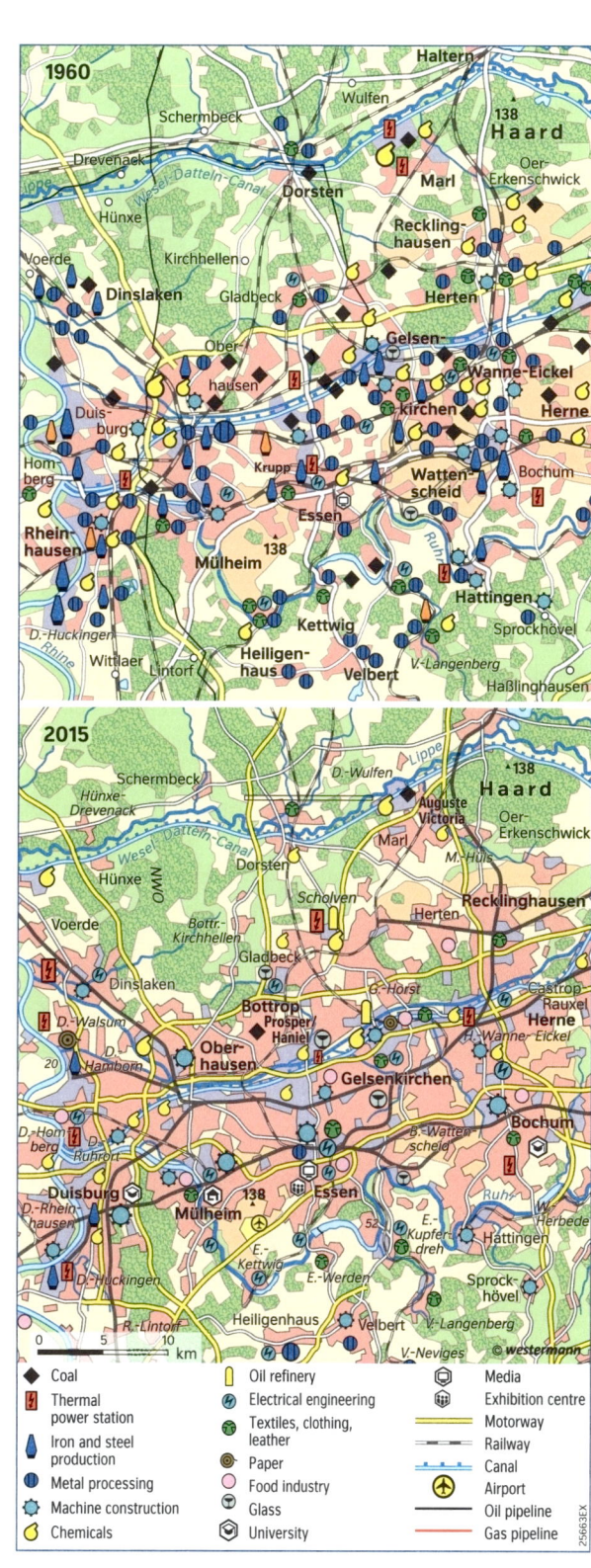

◆ Coal	▯ Oil refinery	⬡ Media
⚡ Thermal power station	⊕ Electrical engineering	⬡ Exhibition centre
▮ Iron and steel production	✿ Textiles, clothing, leather	═ Motorway
◉ Metal processing	◎ Paper	┄ Railway
✺ Machine construction	○ Food industry	✈ Airport
◔ Chemicals	⬡ Glass	── Oil pipeline
	⬡ University	── Gas pipeline

M1 Industries and services in the Ruhr area

3 Explain how the differences that can be seen in **M1** are caused by the development in the German coal industry.

Structural Change in the Ruhr Area

Case study – Dortmund-Hörde

Besides hard coal and brewery, the steel industry had been shaping life in Dortmund-Hörde for about 160 years. There were two industrial areas: Phoenix-West was the location of blast furnaces, in Phoenix-East, steel mills dominated. In-between, there was what is sometimes called "Old-Hörde". In 2001, the last steel mill closed. Some of the furnaces and the mill were subsequently sold to China, marking the end of the iron and steel industry in Dortmund-Hörde.

M1 The end of iron and steel

The development of Dortmund-Hörde after the end of the iron and steel industry included several projects and many different processes: the main aim is to connect different parts of life within the same urban area. Phoenix-West has been developing into an international centre of micro- and nanotechnologies providing around 15,000 jobs for people moving into the newly designed residential area and apartment buildings. The most sought-after living space centres on Phoenix-Lake, the recreational hotspot of the city's renewal-process.

M2 Combining work and life

[...] Am Ende wird man rund um den Phoenix-See nicht nur [...] spazieren, radeln und skaten können, sondern auch arbeiten, wohnen, einkaufen und in einem Restaurant-Boot speisen. [...]
Die Bevölkerungsstruktur im Stadtteil werde sich nun nach und nach verändern, glaubt der Yachtclub-Chef, der selbst im Schatten des ehemaligen Hochofens zur Schule ging. Das werde aber eine Generation dauern: "So schnell sterben die Hoesch-Arbeiter ja nicht aus." Gut möglich, dass die reichen Neu-Hörder den Alt-Bewohnern des Stadtteils später ein Dorn im Auge sind. "Aber wenn mir jeder leidtun würde, der kein Geld für ein Boot hat ...", sagt Krumnacker und lässt den Satz unvollendet. Er hält den See für einen Gewinn für die ganze Stadt, von der letztlich auch die profitieren, die kein Geld haben – selbst wenn sie möglicherweise irgendwann die steigenden Mieten im Stadtteil nicht mehr bezahlen können: "So ist das eben."

Source: www.kulturwest.de (Katrin Pinetzki, gekürzt)

M3 Dortmund am See

❶ Give a short overview of the development in Dortmund-Hörde.

❷ Explain positive and negative effects of the structural change in Dortmund-Hörde.

❸ Compare this example with the structural change in Oberhausen.

pp. 32-33
Texts

Metropolitan Region Rhine-Main

A sightseeing tour through the city centre of Frankfurt/Main

M1 Selected tourist hot spots of Frankfurt – Römer, Paulskirche, Main Tower

1 Collect information to introduce these sites to students from London. Use the Internet and fill in the table.

Category	Information
Paulskirche	
Römer	
Dom	
Alte Oper	
Goethe-Haus	
Main Tower	

2 Mark a tour through Frankfurt including at least the sights from task 1 in the map **M2**. Use your atlas.

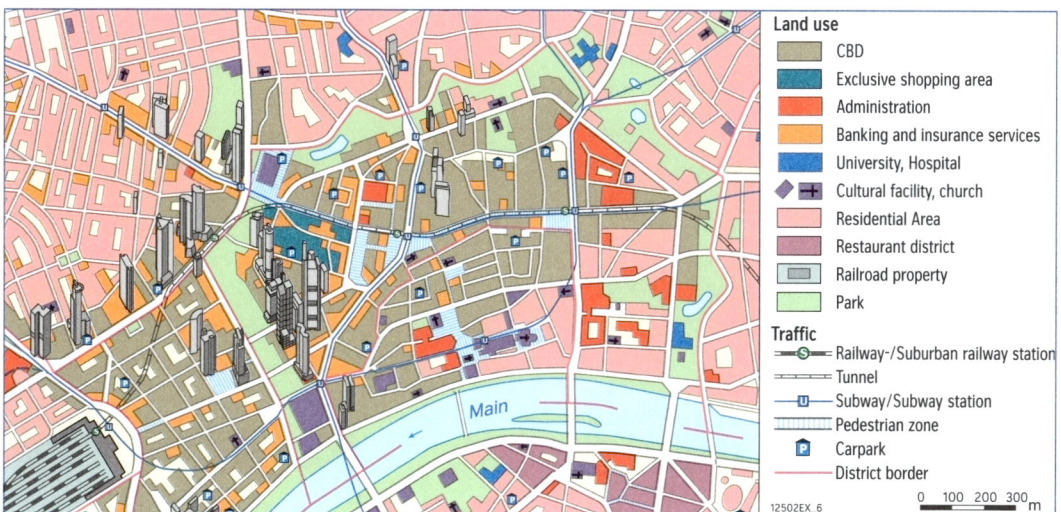

Land use
- CBD
- Exclusive shopping area
- Administration
- Banking and insurance services
- University, Hospital
- Cultural facility, church
- Residential Area
- Restaurant district
- Railroad property
- Park

Traffic
- Railway-/Suburban railway station
- Tunnel
- Subway/Subway station
- Pedestrian zone
- Carpark
- District border

0 100 200 300 m

12502EX_6

M2 The city centre of Frankfurt/Main

 100800-044, -045 schueler.diercke.de

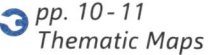 *pp. 10-11 Thematic Maps*

Munich – A Success Story

Working in Munich, living next to Munich

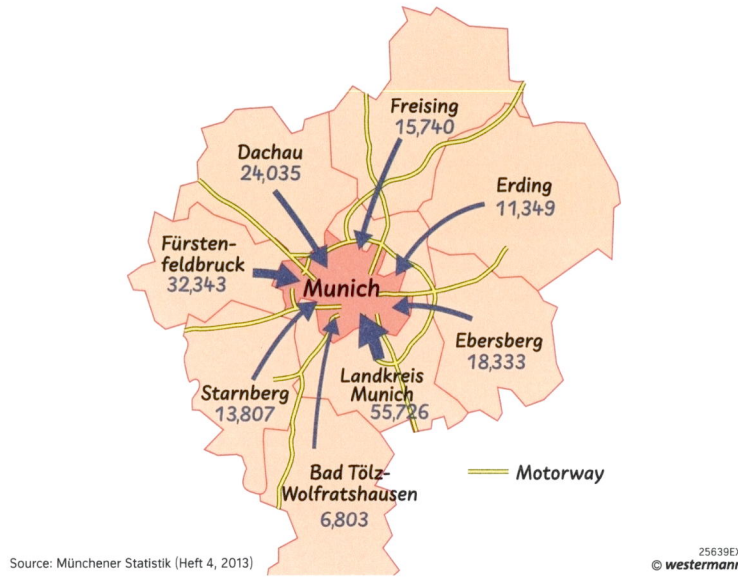

Source: Münchener Statistik (Heft 4, 2013)

25639EX
© **westermann**

M1 Commuting to Munich from the suburban area

Year	Munich	Suburban area
1950	830,833	573,150
1961	1,085,067	629,270
1971	1,293,599	780,645
1987	1,185,421	1,023,314
2014	1,424,604	1,371,088
		Source: Planungsregion 14

M2 Population development

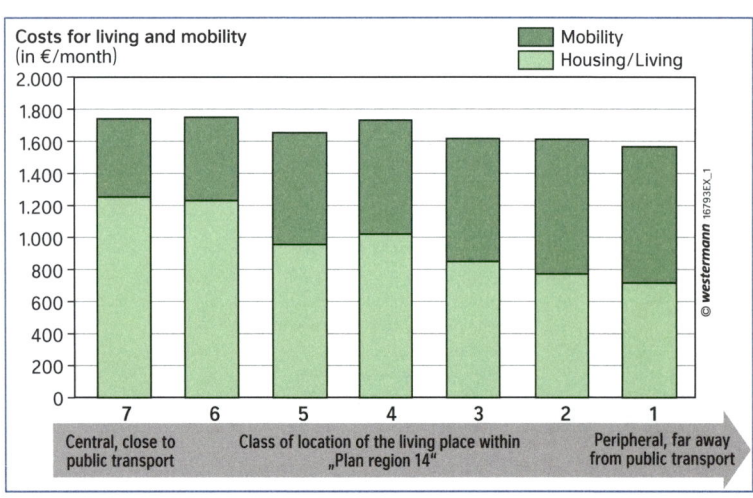

M3 Prices for housing and commuting

❶ Describe the population development of Munich and the Munich region (**M2**).

_____

_____

_____

_____

_____

_____

_____

_____

_____

_____

❷ Explain the importance of commuting in the Munich region (**M1**, **M3**). Use your textbook as well.

_____

_____

_____

_____

_____

_____

_____

_____

_____

_____

100800-051
schueler.diercke.de

➲ pp. 20 - 21
Bar Charts

➲ pp. 34 - 35
Explain

Shrinkage and Growth in the Halle-Leipzig Region

A class from a school in Leipzig is preparing to welcome students from London, who are going to visit Leipzig and other parts of Saxony. To get to know what the British students are interested in visiting, they were asked to note questions about the Halle-Leipzig Region. Here are the questions of the London students:

❶ Fill in possible answers.

Structure	Answer
1. How many people live in Saxony and in your town? What about changes in the number of people?	
2. Which traditional industrial branches are there?	
3. Which important changes in the infrastructure have taken place in your region since the 1990s?	
4. Which examples of growth would you recommend to visit?	
5. Which opportunities for recreation do we have in your region?	

❷ Give a survey about main changes in the area presented in the maps (**M1**).

Structure	Changes
Mining	
Energy production	
Manufacturing industry	
Services	
Infrastructure	
Environment	

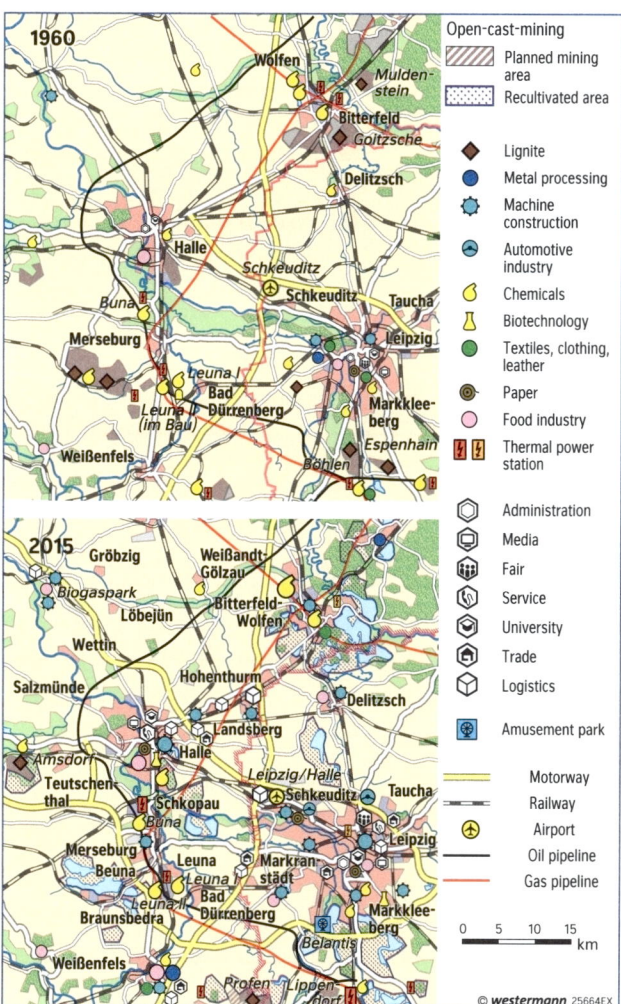

M1 Industries and services in the Leipzig region

Creative young Brits are quitting London for affordable Berlin

More and more burnt-out Londoners are embracing[1] the laid-back cool living of the German capital.

The building that houses Agora, tucked away in a small side-street in residential Neukölln, in an old lock-making factory, is easy to ignore. Outside a handful of people in their late twenties and early thirties are smoking, working on their MacBook Airs, chatting. On the short walk from the front gate to the front door snippets of three different conversations in English can be heard. Inside is a sea of laptops on desks, [...] and a daily changing menu, written in English; a woman with a strong German accent orders a coffee in English, because the woman behind the counter doesn't speak German.

Dani Berg manages Agora's "food platform" (which includes pop-ups and "performance series"), as well as the cafe. She moved to Berlin just over a year ago, after spending a decade in London. "The first time I visited Berlin was eight years ago. People told us not to come to the district I now work and live in, Neukölln, as it was considered to be dangerous, and it wasn't even in the guidebooks or anything. Now it's filled with tourists and expats." [...] Agora is one of many "co-working hubs" that have sprung up in the city, created for the ever-growing startup community. Agora is one of many expat[2] bubbles, catering to the ever-growing number of digital nomads. Berg is well aware that she and the people surrounding her are contributing to the change that Berlin is currently undergoing, something that some Berliners aren't too pleased about. "Occasionally, you get, 'What are you doing here, you're ruining everything,' when people overhear you speaking English. I do feel bad about it, all the time; I'm part of the problem, doing to Berlin what forced me out of London." [...]

Berliners are noticing how rapidly the city is growing and changing, and how much rents are increasing. [...] Scott van Looy, a technical architect from the East End of London, moved to Berlin in 2012 to work for a British company. [...] "The problem is this: people like myself are moving over from London, and snatching up[3] flats swiftly after seeing what they think is a bargain. But in reality what we perceive to be a bargain is still an inflated price for locals, so prices are being driven up." [...]

Source: www.theguardian.com (08 Apr 2015)

M1 Excerpt from a newspapers article

HELPFUL WORDS
for M1:
1 – sich begeistern
2 – Auswanderer
3 – zugreifen

❶ Read the article and underline indications for the process of gentrification.

❷ Write a dialogue in German or English between a Londoner and a Berliner – both living in Berlin-Neukölln – in which they discuss the process of gentrification.

_____   _____

_____   _____

_____   _____

_____   _____

_____   _____

_____   _____

_____   _____

_____   _____

Germany in a Changing World

Taking Notes During Talks and when Watching Videos

Note-taking is a very important technique, not only during a talk or presentation given by your teachers or peers but also when watching videos.

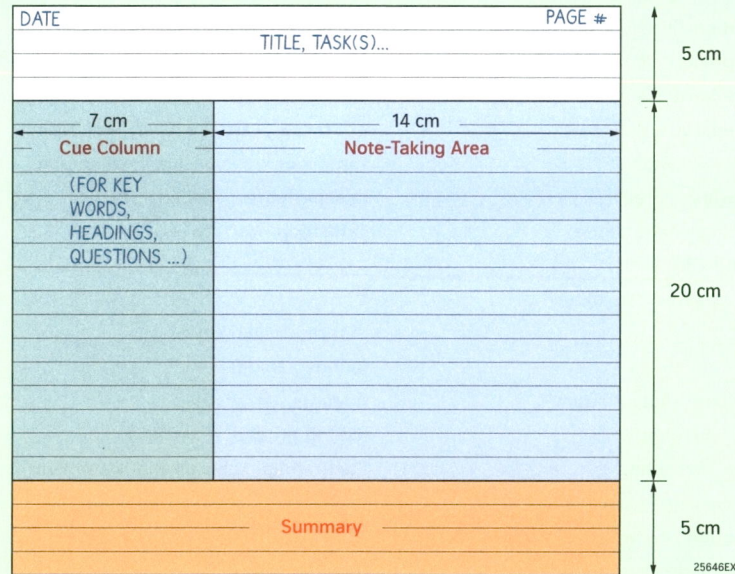

M1 Arrangement of note-taking paper

Ideally you watch a video in your own time. Watch it several times, adding to your notes. Use the subtitle function when available. (Caution: In some videos the subtitles are not correct.) When watching videos, jot down the time of the video passed for later reference.

If the video is available online, http://www.videonot.es/ can assist you taking notes. It is advisable to create an email account especially for this purpose.

Types of videos:
animated film (cartoon), broadcast, docudrama, documentary, feature film, film clip, motion picture, (news) report, TV coverage

STEPS

STEP 1 – Preparation:
An established arrangement of a note-taking page is shown in **M1**. If you are given an observatory task in advance, write it down at the top of the page along with given key words in the cue column. If there are several tasks, use a new page for each task.

STEP 2 – Note-taking during the talk:
Use the note-taking column (**M1**). Use telegraphic sentences, symbols, and abbreviations (**M2**) to speed up note-taking. Bullet points or numbering for a clear structure. Leave space for further additions.

STEP 3 – Note review:
After the talk or when the video is over, go through your notes to add things, underline, colour-mark, connect, or cross out unnecessary information. Use the space at the bottom of each page for a summary.

STEP 4 – Questions:
In a different pen colour, formulate questions in the cue column, based on your notes. Writing questions helps to clarify meanings, reveal relationships, establish continuity, and strengthen your memory. Check if you can solve the tasks which were given to you before the talk/video.

STEP 5 – Revise:
Looking at the tasks, questions or key words in the left column only, answer the questions, facts, or ideas indicated by the key words in your own words. A good way to revise is to write several multiple choice questions about the subject for your peers.

+	and, add, plus	ea	each
=	is, are	min	minimum, least
≈	about, approximately	max	maximum, most
>	more than	qty.	quantity (amount)
<	less than	N.B.	note well
#	number	eg	for example
x	times	ie	that is
→	leads to, causes	b4	before
←	comes from, caused by	p	before
↔	compared to, exchanges	f	after
/	or, pee	w/	with
↑	increase, grow, gain	wo	without
↓	decrease, loss	re	regarding
♀	femal, woman, girl	b/c	because
♂	male, man, boy	s/t	some-thing
yrs	years	d/f	different
@	at	govt	govern-ment
!!	important	prbs	problems

M2 Abbreviations and symbols for note-taking

Words

A

abandoned   aufgegeben, verlassen

to **abandon something**   etwas verlassen

to **abolish**   abschaffen, verwerfen

access   Zugang

to **accomplish**   erreichen, vollbringen

to **account for something**   ausmachen, darstellen

to **achieve**   erreichen, erzielen

achievement   Errungenschaft

to **adapt**   anpassen

to **adopt**   annehmen, übernehmen, einführen

advantage   Vorteil

to **advocate something**   befürworten

agrarian-oriented   landwirtschaftlich geprägt

aid   Hilfe

aid agency   Hilfsorganisation

all-day school   Ganztagsschule

allocation   Zuweisung, Verteilung, Vergabe

annually   jährlich

to **absorb**   absorbieren

applicant   Bewerber

arable land   Ackerfläche

aspiration   Bestreben

to **assign**   zuweisen

average   durchschnittlich, Durchschnitts-

B

to **badmouth**   beschimpfen

bankruptcy   Konkurs, Pleite

to **benefit**   profitieren

biocapacity   Biokapazität

bland   fade, geschmacklos

blast furnace   Hochofen

to **boom**   florieren, boomen

brewery   Brauerei

C

to **calculate**   berechnen

to **characterise**   charakterisieren, beschreiben

chasm   Kluft

child labour   Kinderarbeit

childbearing age   gebärfähiges Alter

to **churn out**   ausstoßen

to **cite**   nennen, anführen

coalification   Verkohlung

to **collapse**   zusammenbrechen

commitment   Verpflichtung, Verbindlichkeit

community   Kommune, Gemeinde

to **commute**   pendeln

commuting   Pendeln

to **compare**   vergleichen

concerning   betreffend

confluence   Zusammenfluss

conglomerate   Mischkonzern

conservation   Bewahrung, Schutz

to **consider**   betrachten

construction   Bau, Errichtung

consumption   Verbrauch

contraceptives   Verhütungsmittel

corporate farm   Genossenschaftsfarm

corrugated iron   Wellblech

covering   Verkleidung

craft brewery   Brauerei

crèche   Kindertagesstätte

to **crumble**   zerfallen

current   gegenwärtig, aktuell

D

day of expiry   Ablaufdatum

decade   Jahrzehnt

to **declare**   erklären

decline   Sinken, Rückgang

deforestation   Entwaldung

delight   Freude, Vergnügen

department store   Kaufhaus

departure   Abreise

dependent   abhängig

to **depict**   abbilden, darstellen

depopulation   Entvölkerung

desperate   verzweifelt

development   Entwicklung

discrimination   Diskriminierung

disparity   Unterschied

disposal   Beseitigung

dispute   Streit

disruption   Störung, Unterbrechung

to **dissolve**   auflösen

distance   Entfernung, Abstand

distribution   Verteilung

to **dominate**   dominieren, vorherrschen

downtown   Innenstadt, Stadtzentrum

to **draw**   zeichnen

to **drown**   ertrinken

to **dumb**   das geistige Niveau senken

E

ecological deficit   ökologisches Defizit

ecological footprint   ökologischer Fußabdruck

ecological overshot   ökologische Überbelastung

ecological reserve   ökologische Reserve

economy   Wirtschaft

to **emerge**   entstehen

emission   Emission

to **employ**   beschäftigen

employee   Mitarbeiter, Arbeitnehmer

employment structure   Beschäftigtenstruktur

equality   Gleichberechtigung, Gleichheit

equalling   gleichend, entsprechend

to **escape**   entkommen

estimate   Schätzung

eventually   schließlich

excerpt   Exzerpt, Ausschnitt, Auszug

exhaust system   Abgassystem

existence   Existenz, Bestehen, Dasein

expansion   Expansion, Erweiterung

to **experience**   erleben, erfahren

extinction   Aussterben

F

to **face**   begegnen

famine   Hungersnot

findings   Ergebnisse

fishing ground   Fangplatz

fluctuating   schwankend, veränderlich

for good   endgültig, für immer

foreign   ausländisch

fortune   Glück

founding   Gründung

fragmentation   Fragmentierung, Zersplitterung

G

garbage patch   Müllstrudel

gearbox   Getriebe

to **generate**   erzeugen, erwirtschaften

to **gentrify**   aufwerten

glazier's workshop   Glaserei

global   weltweit

global city   Globale Stadt

globalisation   Globalisierung

gradually   schrittweise, allmählich

graduation   Schulabschluss

grain   Getreide

grocery store   Lebensmittelgeschäft

Gross National Product (GNP)   Bruttonationaleinkommen

H

harvest   Ernte

hedge   Hecke

I

impact   Auswirkung

impetus   Antrieb, Impuls

in favour of   für, zugunsten von

incentive   Anreiz

income   Einkommen

increase   Steigerung, Zunahme

indicator   Indikator, Kennzeichen

infant mortality   Kindersterblichkeit

intrinsically tied to   untrennbar verbunden mit

investment   Investition

irrigation   Bewässerung

L

to label beschriften, kennzeichnen
labour Arbeit
lack of Mangel an
land reclamation Landgewinnung
land sealing Versiegelung des Landes
landed gentry Landeigentümer
large-scale großangelegt
latter letzte
leisure time Freizeit
life expectancy Lebenserwartung
literacy rate Alphabetisierungsrate
livelihood Lebensgrundlage
lorry Lastkraftwagen (Lkw)
to lure ködern, anziehen

M

to maintain erhalten, pflegen
manufacturer Hersteller, Produzent
marital age Heiratsalter
medical advances medizinische Fortschritte
menace Bedrohung, Gefahr
midtown Innenstadtrand
momentous bedeutsam, folgenschwer
municipality Gemeinde, Kommune
myth Mythos, Märchen

N

native einheimisch
to neglect vernachlässigen
neighbourhood Nachbarschaft, Umgebung
to numb betäuben
nutrient Nährstoff

O

to observe beobachten
to obtain erhalten, beziehen
occupied besetzt
to occupy besetzen
offshore küstennah, der Küste vorgelagert
outbreak Ausbruch
overfishing Überfischung

P

per capita pro Kopf
pharmaceuticals Arzneimittel
physician Arzt
to pick pflücken
pillar Säule, Pfeiler, Stütze
to plead bitten, flehen
plumbing Rohrleitung
point of view Sichtweise, Blickwinkel
points of interest Sehenswürdigkeiten
to pollute something verschmutzt
to ponder erwägen, nachdenken
poor arm

population Bevölkerung
portfolio Bestand, Portfolio
to possess something besitzen
to pour gießen
to preserve erhalten
previous vorhergehende
processed verarbeitet
to project something etwas vorhersagen
property Eigentum, Besitz
proximity Nähe

R

radiator Kühler
to raise awareness to ein Bewusstsein für etwas Wecken
real estate Immobilie
real-estate prices Immobilienpreise
reasonable akzeptabel, angemessen, vertretbar
to receive erhalten
recreation Erholung
to recycle aufbereiten
to reduce reduzieren
to refuse ablehnen, ausschlagen
regardless gleichgültig
reindustrialisation Wiedererstarken von Industrie
to replace ersetzen
to represent ausmachen, darstellen
representative Vertreter
reputation Ruf
to require erfordern, verlangen
resident Einwohner, Bewohner
retail Einzelhandel
retail outlet Einzelhandelsgeschäft
to reuse wiederverwenden
rich reich
row Reihe
rubber Kautschuk
rural ländlich

S

saviour Retter, Heiland
seemingly scheinbar
seepage Versickernde Flüssigkeit
separate getrennt, einzeln
sewage Abwasser
shack Bude
share Anteil
sought-after begehrt, gesucht
sparingly sparsam
to spread verbreiten
to spur beleben, anregen
structural change Strukturwandel
to stumble stolpern

subcontractor Zulieferer
subsequently anschließend
subsidies Subventionen, Fördermittel, Zuschüsse
suburb Vorort
suburban area Stadtrandgebiet
to suffer erleiden
to suggest empfehlen
to support unterstützen
surplus Überschuss, Überangebot
suspension Aufhängung
sustainability Nachhaltigkeit
swamp Sumpf

T

thermal power station Wärmekraftwerk
threat Bedrohung, Gefahr
timber Holz
Total Fertility Rate (TFR) Gesamtfruchtbarkeitsrate
trade Handel
trade flow Handelsverkehr
trip Reise
trouble Ärger

U

uncultivated nicht bewirtschaftet
to undergo etwas durchmachen, durchleben
undermining untergrabend
unemployment rate Arbeitslosenquote
unfamiliar ungewohnt
unskilled ungelernt
unrest Aufruhr

V

vacant frei, leerstehend
value Wert, Wertigkeit
vast riesig, enorm

W

to wane abnehmen
waste arising Müllaufkommen
waste facilities Abfallentsorgungsanlage
wasted verschwendet
wastewater Abwasser
water conservation Gewässerschutz
whereas während, wohingegen
windbreak Windschutz
wiring loom Kabelbaum

Starthilfen

S. 6, Aufgabe 1
Sieh dir die Daten erst genau an und entscheide, welche Diagrammform die geeignete ist. Die entsprechende Methodenseite findest du im 'Toolkit'.

S. 9, Aufgabe 1
Gehe vom Begriff in der Mitte aus und stelle dir die entsprechende Situation in der Entstehung eines Smartphones vor. Frage dich: Welche Aspekte sind an dieser Stelle besonders wichtig?

S. 11, Aufgabe 2
Achte auf die Erklärungen zu den Punkten in **M1** und denke in Zusammenhängen.
Wie sind die Arbeitsbedingungen? Welche Ausbildung wird benötigt? Wo wird viel und wo weniger Geld an einem Smartphone verdient? Wie sind die Lebensbedingungen in den orange markierten Ländern im Allgemeinen zu charakterisieren?

S. 15, Aufgabe 1
Unterscheide zwischen ökologischen und wirtschaftlichen Folgen. Das hilft dir, den Überblick zu behalten.

S. 24, Aufgabe 1
Sieh dir die Daten erst genau an und entscheide, welche Diagrammform die geeignete ist. Die entsprechende Methodenseite findest du im 'Toolkit'.

S. 25, Aufgabe 2a
Berechne: percentage / 100 * total Mtoe = Mtoe für den Energieträger.
Beispiel für "Kohle, 2005":
28.61/100*11,355 = 3,248.6655, gerundet 3,249 Mtoe.

S. 26, Aufgabe 1
Beispiel für plant cellulose: 10/34 * 100 = 29.4 %

S. 28, Aufgabe 1
1. What exactly does the text **M1** suggest?
2. What are the pros and cons of increased use (fracking, environmental issues)?
3. What is my opinion?

S. 32, Aufgabe 3
Beachte, dass Energietransport aufwändig und teuer ist. Wähle zwei Standorte nahe von Industrieregionen.

S. 33, Aufgabe 3
Konzentriere dich auf die positiven Auswirkungen für Ägypten und die Probleme im Energietransport. Bereite Lösungsvorschläge vor.

S. 35, Aufgabe 3
Sammle Argumente für und gegen einen Anstieg der Produktionskosten. Berücksichtige neue Technologien, die auf verschiedenen Seiten des Textbooks präsentiert werden.

S. 41, Aufgabe 1
Beachte die Checkliste auf Seite 18 im Workbook.

S. 45, Aufgabe 1
Erinnere dich: Klimadiagramme kombinieren ebenfalls ein Balken und ein Liniendiagramm.
Tipp: Benutze unterschiedliche Farben um deutlich zu machen, zu welcher Achse die jeweiligen Daten gehören.

S. 48, Aufgabe 3
Es empfiehlt sich, hier die Bevölkerungszahlen im Textbuch (S.109: **M3**) als Grundlage für die Beantwortung der Frage heranzuziehen.

S. 50, Aufgabe 1
Achte auf mögliche Zusammenhänge und Beziehungen zwischen den einzelnen Förderthemen.

S. 52, Aufgabe 3
Berücksichtigt der geplante Tunnel gleichmäßig Ansprüche aus Wirtschaft, Natur und Gesellschaft?

S. 59, Aufgabe 1
Vergiss nicht, die Kreisdiagramme in verschiedenen Größen zu zeichnen, da sich die Gesamtzahl der Gastarbeiter zwischen 1965 und 1973 auch verändert hat.

S. 68, Aufgabe 2
Du solltest dich auf maximal zwei Punkte bei der Diskussion konzentrieren.

Sources

adpic Bildagentur, Köln: 65 M1 re. (R. Naumann); African Clean Energy (Pty) Ltd, Maseru: 31 M2; alamy images, Abingdon/Oxfordshire: 13 M1 (David Hodges); CartoonStock.com, Bath: 41 M1 (Clive Goddard); dreamstime.com, Brentwood: 65 M1 li. (Maria Feklistova); Fachagentur Nachwachsende Rohstoffe e.V. (FNR), Gülzow-Prüzen: 60 M1; fotolia.com, New York: 38 M1 (Boggy), 38 M2 (Johan Larson), 65 M1 m. (Kristan); Google Maps: 8 M1 (Satellite Image); iStockphoto.com, Calgary: 24 M2 (vlad_karavaev); Picture-Alliance, Frankfurt/M.: 61 M1 m. (Helga Lade); Rieger, Anja, Backnang: alle Illus Stifte; Shutterstock.com, New York: Titel (RomanSlavik.com), 64 M1 (Bildagentur Zoonar); Tönnies, Uwe , Laatzen: 61 M1 li.; toonpool.com, Berlin, Castrop-Rauxel: 18 M1 (Popa Matumula); ullstein bild, Berlin: 61 M1 re.; Visum Foto, Hannover: 15 M1 (Jesco Denzel).

Appendix